Essential Node.js Security

for ExpressJS Web Applications

Liran Tal

Essential Node.js Security
for ExpressJS Web Applications

Liran Tal

ISBN 978-1-365-69855-2

This is a Leanpub book. Leanpub empowers authors and publishers with the Lean Publishing process. Lean Publishing is the act of publishing an in-progress ebook using lightweight tools and many iterations to get reader feedback, pivot until you have the right book and build traction once you do.

This work is licensed under a Creative Commons Attribution-NonCommercial-NoDerivs 3.0 Unported License

Tweet This Book!

Please help Liran Tal by spreading the word about this book on Twitter!

The suggested tweet for this book is:

I'm reading up on Essential Node.js Security for ExpressJS Web Applications by Liran Tal #nodejs #javascript #npm

The suggested hashtag for this book is #securenodejs.

Find out what other people are saying about the book by clicking on this link to search for this hashtag on Twitter:

https://twitter.com/search?q=#securenodejs

Contents

Foreword i

About The Author iii
    Liran Tal iii

About The Reviewers v
    Danny Grander v
    Tim Kadlec v
    Cody B. Daig v
    Zach Sosana v

About The Book vii
    Source Code vii

HTTP Headers Security 1
    Node.js Packages to Secure The HTTP Transport 1
    Strict Transport Security 3
    X-Frame-Options 6
    Content-Security-Policy 9
    Other HTTP headers 14
    Summary 16

Secure Session Management 17
    Session Security Risks 17
    Session Security in Node.js and ExpressJS 18
    Summary 23

Hardening ExpressJS 25
    Security Through Obscurity 25
    Brute-Force Protection 25
    Advanced Functionality Limiting 27
    body-parser middleware 28
    Summary 30

CONTENTS

Cross-Site Request Forgery (CSRF) 31
- The Risk 31
- The Solution 33
- Summary 41

Cross-Site Scripting (XSS) 43
- The Risk 44
- The Solution 45
- Summary 50

Secure Code Guidelines 51
- The Risk 51
- Input Validation 51
- Output Encoding 53
- Regular Expressions 55
- Strict Mode and Eval 60
- Cryptographic Practices 61
- User Process Privileges 64
- Summary 66

Injection Flaws 67
- NoSQL Injections 67
- NoSQL SSJS Injections 71
- Blind NoSQL Injections 73
- OS Command Injection 75
- Summary 77

Secure Dependency Management 79
- Evaluating Dependencies 80
- Dependency Tracking 83
- NPM Shrinkwrap 91

Yarn as npm Package Management 93
- Characteristics of Yarn 93
- Command Line Usage 94
- Installing Yarn 94
- Tracking Dependencies with Yarn 94
- Summary 95

About The Author

Liran Tal

Liran is actively maintaining and contributing to major open source projects in the areas of JavaScript and Node.js. He takes a lead role in maintaining and developing the MEAN.JS project, and is a top contributor to the MEAN.io full stack JavaScript framework too. He is a seasoned speaker in JavaScript and Node.js events, including the recent OWASP AppSec IL 2016 event with a talk about Node.js Security.

At Hewlett Packard Enterprise, Liran Tal is leading the R&D engineering team for HPE Software's enterprise content market place, distribution, and collaboration platform featuring the MEAN technology stack with AngularJS, Node.js, MongoDB and a Java REST API backend. He plays a key technical role in system architecture design, shaping the technology strategy from planning and development to deployment and maintenance in HPE IaaS cloud.

Being an avid supporter and contributor to the open source movement, in 2007 he has redefined network RADIUS management by founding, and developing daloRADIUS, a world-recognized and industry-leading open source project (http://www.daloradius.com).

Liran graduated cum laude in his Bachelor of Business and Information Systems Analysis studies and enjoys spending his time with his beloved wife Tal, and his magical son Ori. Amongst other things, his hobbies include playing the guitar, hacking all things Linux, and continuously experimenting and contributing to open source, and web development projects.

About The Reviewers

Danny Grander

Danny Grander is a veteran security researcher and the cofounder of Snyk.io, where he works on open source security and leads Snyk's security research. Previously, Danny was the CTO of Gita and a lead researcher and developer for a few startups. Danny's CTF team, Pasten, won both the Chaos Computer Club and Google's CTFs.

Tim Kadlec

Tim is head of developer relations at Snyk—a company focused on making open source code more secure. He is the author of Implementing Responsive Design: Building sites for an anywhere, everywhere web, and was a contributing author for High Performance Images, Smashing Book #4: New Perspectives on Web Design, and the Web Performance Daybook Volume 2.

Cody B. Daig

Cody is a technical mentor at Hack Reactor where he teaches students software engineering in a remote immersive bootcamp. Previously, he has worked as a developer in the 3D printing and affiliate marketing industry. He is currently active with the MEAN.js open source project on GitHub. You can find him on twitter @codydaig or on his website at www.codydaig.me.

Zach Sosana

Zach is a passionate Web and Mobile Hacker (JavaScript Software Development Engineer), team lead and mentor at War Room labs where he works on open sourcery and enterprise projects. A web & mobile app coding enthusiast and lover of all things JavaScript. You can find him on twitter @thesosana or on his github profile at www.github.com/SOSANA/.

About The Book

This book is intended to be a hands-on thorough guide for securing web applications based on Node.js and the ExpressJS web application framework. Many of the concepts, tools and practices in this book are primarily based on open source libraries and the author leverages these projects and highlights them.

The main objective of the book is to equip the reader with practical solutions to real world problems, and so this book is heavily saturated with source code examples as well as a high level description of the risks involved with any security topic, and the practical solution to prevent or mitigate it.

Even though ExpressJS is chosen as the case for web application framework, many concepts in this book can, and should be taken into account, and implemented with any other framework. Concepts like *secure code*, *nosql injections*, *secure session management* and others are important security topics and would benefit any Node.js developer whose primary focus is web development.

Source Code

All the source code examples, and many more variations of them can be found in their complete setup and form in the following GitHub repository inside the *code/* directory https://github.com/lirantal/nodejssecurity

Feedback and comments are highly appreciated and welcome. If you find any issues, improvements, or room for updates please open a GitHub issue or Pull-Request.

---

[3] https://github.com/lirantal/nodejssecurity

HTTP Headers Security

Developing web applications means that our program rides on communication protocols which already set standards for how to transfer data and how to manage it.

Browsers utilize HTTP headers to enforce and confirm such communication standards as well as security policies. Making use of these HTTP headers to increase security for our clients (web browsers) is a very efficient and quick method to mitigate and prevent many security vulnerabilities.

Node.js Packages to Secure The HTTP Transport

Let's review two libraries which we can use to implement these security related HTTP headers and apply the solution required for each security mechanism that we will be reviewing:

- Lusca
- Helmet

Helmet

Helmet[4] is a pluggable library for ExpressJS which provides a wide range of solutions related to the transport security layer, such as Cross-Site-Scripting (XSS) security, X-Frame protection and many others.

Helmet, being a collection of transport security libraries, is well maintained and kept up to date. As such, it makes a good choice to incorporate in your enterprise or production apps.

More on Helmet

Helmet has been around originally since 2012 and is considered matured and production-ready with stable releases and adoption by many frameworks and Node.js projects. It is mainly developed by Evan Hahn, and Adam Baldwin who maintain some dozen npm packages and are very actively involved in ExpressJS and other Node.js projects on GitHub.

Helmet's libraries work by introducing middlewares for ExpressJS which can respond to requests being served by an ExpressJS application.

---

[4]https://github.com/helmetjs/helmet

Lusca

Lusca[5] is another library to help secure the HTTP transport layer, similar to Helmet, and provides a collection of configurable options to add protection for risks related to Cross-Site-Request-Forgery (CSRF), Content-Security-Policy, and others.

Lusca integrates with ExpressJS web applications using a middleware implementation to mitigate some of the HTTP transport layer vulnerabilities. It is mainly developed and maintained by team members from PayPal who officialy sponsor the work on this library, currently lead by Jean-Charles Sisk.

 Security-oriented frameworks

Lusca is a library that is part of a bigger web application framework called kraken.js[6] that focuses on security first, and is too, officially maintained by PayPal's own people.

---

[5] https://github.com/krakenjs/lusca
[6] https://github.com/krakenjs/kraken-js

Strict Transport Security

Strict Transport Security, also known as HSTS, is a protocol standard to enforce secure connections to the server via HTTP over SSL/TLS. HSTS is configured and transmitted from the server to any HTTP web client using the HTTP header *Strict-Transport-Security* which specifies a time interval during which the web client should only communicate over an HTTP secured connection (HTTPS).

Tip

When a *Strict-Transport-Security* header is sent over HTTP the web client ignores it because the connection is unsecured to begin with.

The Risk

The risks that may arise when communicating over a secure HTTPS connection is that a malicious user can perform an Man-In-The-Middle (MITM) attack and down-grade future requests to the web server to use an HTTP connection, thus being able to sniff and read all the data that flows through.

Interesting fact:

The original HSTS draft[7] was published in 2011 by Jeff Hodges from PayPal, Collin Jackson from Carnegie Mellon University, and Adam Barth from Google.

Sending HTTP requests to the web server even though an HTTPS connection was initially made is not a problem on its own, as the user is unaware of why this is happening and wouldn't necessarily suspect. Perhaps the server has a REST endpoint which is not yet HTTPS-supported?

In the following flow diagram, *Figure 1-1*, we can see an example scenario where the server returns an HTML file for the login page to the browser, which includes some resources that are accessible over HTTP, like the submit button's image.

If an attacker is able to perform a Man-In-The-Middle attack and "sit on the wire" to listen and sniff any un-encrypted traffic that flows through, then they can essentially access and read those HTTP requests which include sensitive data such as the user's cookie. Even worse scenarios may include HTTP resources set for POST or PUT endpoints where actual data is being sent and can be sniffed.

---

[7] https://tools.ietf.org/html/rfc6797

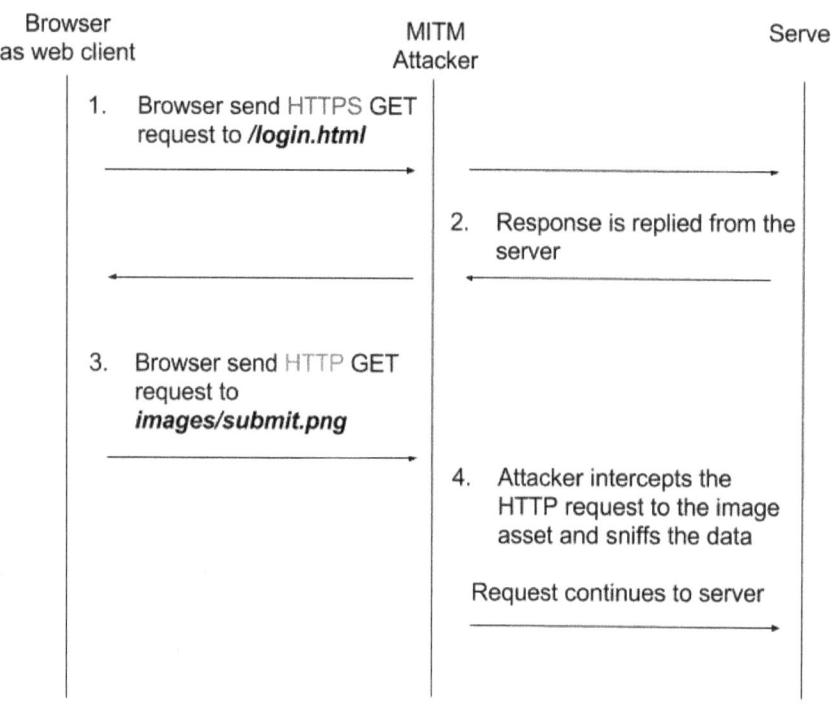

Figure 1-1 - Visualizing HTTPS MITM Attack

The Solution

When web servers want to protect their web clients through a secured HTTPS connection, they need to send the *Strict-Transport-Security* header with a given value which represents the duration of time in seconds which the web client should send future requests over a secured HTTPS connection.

e.g. telling the web client to send further secure HTTPS requests for the next hour:

```
Strict-Transport-Security: max-age=3600
```

Helmet Implementation

To use Helmet's HSTS library we need to download the npm package and we will also add it as a package dependency to the Node.js project we're working on:

```
1  npm install helmet --save
```

Let's setup the hsts middleware to indicate web client such as a browser that it should only send HTTPS requests to our server's hostname for the next 1 month:

```
1  var helmet = require('helmet');
2
3  // Set the expiration time of HTTPS requests to the server to 1 month,
4  // specified in milliseconds
5  var reqDuration = 2629746000;
6
7  app.use(helmet.hsts({
8    maxAge: reqDuration
9  }));
```

In the above snippet, app is an ExpressJS app object, which we are instructing to use the hsts library.

A quite common case is where web servers also have sub-domains to fetch assets from, or make REST API calls to, in which case we would also like to protect them and enforce HTTPS requests. To do that, we can include the following optional parameter to the hsts options object:

```
1    includeSubDomains: true
```

Lusca Implementation

If Lusca is not yet installed we can install it with npm as follows:

```
1  npm install lusca --save
```

Once lusca is installed, we can set it up for HSTS support with an ExpressJS application setup:

```
1  var lusca = require('lusca');
2
3  // Set the expiration time of HTTPS requests to the server to 1 month,
4  // specified in milliseconds
5  var reqDuration = 2629746000;
6
7  app.use(lusca({
8    hsts: {
9      maxAge: requestsDuration
10   }
11 }));
```

As can be seen, using lusca is very similar to using helmet, including their optional arguments like maxAge, and includeSubDomains.

X-Frame-Options

The X-Frame-Options[8] HTTP header was introduced to mitigate an attack called Clickjacking which allows an attacker to disguise page elements such as buttons, and text inputs by hiding their view behind real web pages which render on the screen using an iframe HTML element, or similar objects.

Deprecation notice

The X-Frame-Options header was never standardized as part of an official specification but many of the popular browsers today still support it. It's successor is the Content-Security-Policy header which will be covered in the next section and one should focus on implementing CSP for new websites being built.

The Risk

Clickjacking[9] attack is about mis-leading the user to perform a seemingly naive and harmless operation while in reality the user is clicking buttons of other elements or typing text into an input field which is under the user's control.

Common examples of employing Clickjacking attack:

1. If a bank, or email account website doesn't employ an X-Frame-Options HTTP header then a malicious attacker can render them on an iframe, and place the attacker's own input fields on the exact location of the bank or email website's input for username and password and to record your credentials information.
2. A web application for video or voice chat that is in-secure can be exploited by this attack to let the user mistakenly assume they are just clicking around on the screen, or playing a game, while in reality a series of clicks are actually turning on your web camera or microphone.

The Solution

To mitigate the problem, a web server can respond to a browser's request with an X-Frame-Options HTTP header which is set to one of the following possible values:

1. DENY - Specifies that the website can not be rendered in an iframe, frame, or object HTML elements.
2. SAMEORIGIN - Specifies that the website can be rendered only if it is requested to be embedded on an iframe, frame or object HTML elements from the same domain.

---

[8]http://tools.ietf.org/html/7034
[9]https://www.owasp.org/index.php/Clickjacking

3. ALLOW-FROM <URI> - Specifies that the website can be framed and rendered from the provided URI value. Important to notice that you can't specify multiple URI values, but are limited to just one.

A few examples to show how this header is set are:

```
1  X-Frame-Options: ALLOW-FROM http://www.mydomain.com
```

and

```
1  X-Frame-Options: DENY
```

Caution of Proxies

Web proxies are often used as a means of caching and they natively perform a lot of headers manipulation. Beware of proxies which may remove this or other security related headers.

Helmet Implementation

With helmet, implementing this header is as simple as requiring the helmet package and using ExpressJS's `app` object to instruct ExpressJS to use the xframe middleware provided by helmet.

Setting the X-Frame-Options to completely deny any frames:

```
1  var helmet = require('helmet');
2
3  app.use(helmet.frameguard({
4    action: 'deny'
5  }));
```

Similarly, we can allow frames to occur only from the same origin by providing the following object:

```
1  {
2    action: 'sameorigin'
3  }
```

Or to allow frames to occur from a specified host:

```
{
  action: 'allow-from',
  domain: 'https://mydomain.com'
}
```

Lusca Implementation

If lusca library is already installed and our ExpressJS application is already configured and provides the app object, then:

```
var lusca = require('lusca');

app.use(lusca({
    xframe: 'SAMEORIGIN'
  }
));
```

Content-Security-Policy

As reviewed before with the X-Frame-Options header, there are many attacks related to content injection in the user's browser whether it is the Clickjacking attack, or other forms of attacks such as Cross-Site-Scripting (XSS).

Another improvement to the previous set of headers is a header which can tell the browser which content to trust so that the browser is able to prevent attempts to disable malicious content injection that is specified not to be trusted by web servers.

With Content-Security-Policy[10] (CSP) it is possible to Â prevent a wide range of attacks, including Cross-site scripting and other content injections, incluing Clickjacking which we already reviewed and in this regard if CSP is implemented then it obsoletes the need to also use the X-Frame-Options header.

The Risk

By default, the CSP header will prevent and mitigate severe issues such as:

- Inline JavaScript code specified with `<script>` tags, and any DOM events which trigger JavaScript execution such as `onClick()` etc.
- Inline CSS code specified via a `<style>` tag or attribute elements

The Solution

With CSP we can whitelist many configurations for trusted content and as such the initial setup can grow to a set of complex directives. Let's review one directive called *connect-src*. It is used to control which remotes the browser is allowed to connect via XHR, or WebSockets. Acceptable values that we can set for this or other directives are:

- *'none'* - not allowing remote calls such as XHR at all
- *'self'* - only allow remote calls to our own domain (an exact domain/hostname. sub-domains aren't allowed)

An example for this directive being set by the web server and allows remote calls only to our own domain and to Google's API domain:

```
Content-Security-Policy: connect-src 'self' https://apis.google.com;
```

---

[10] https://developer.mozilla.org/en-US/docs/Web/Security/CSP/Introducing_Content_Security_Policy

Another directive to control the whitelist for JavaScript sources is called *script-src*. Such directive helps mitigate Cross-Site-Scripting (XSS) attacks by instructing the browser what is valid source for evaluating and executing JavaScript source code.

script-src supports the *'none'* and *'self'* keywords as values, including the following options too:

- *'unsafe-inline'* - allow any inline JavaScript source code such as `<script>`, and DOM events triggering like `onClick()`, or `javascript:` URIs. It is also affecting CSS for inline tags.
- *'unsafe-eval'* - allows executing `eval()` code

For example, a policy for allowing JavaScript to be executed only from our own domain, from Google's, and allows inline JavaScript code as well:

```
1  Content-Security-Policy: script-src 'self' https://apis.google.com 'unsafe-inlin\
2  e'
```

A full list of supported directives can be found on the CSP policy directives page on MDN[11] but let's cover some othert common options and their values.

- *default-src* - where a directive doesn't have a value, it defaults to an open, non-restricting configuration. It's safer to set a default for all of the un-configured options and this is the purpose of the *default-src* directive.
- *script-src* - a directive to set which locations we allow to load or execute JavaScript sources from. If it's set to a value of *'self'* then no inline JavaScript tags are allowed, such as `<script>`, and only sources from our own domain.

 On implementing CSP

It should also be noted that the CSP configuration needs to meet the implementation of your web application architecture so that if you deny inline <script> blocks then your R&D team is aware of this and do not rely on such inline JavaScript code blocks, otherwise you will be breaking features and functionality.

Helmet Implementation

Using helmet we can configure a secured policy for trusted content. Due to the potential for a complex configuration we will review several different policies in smaller blocks of code to easily explain what is happening when we implement CSP.

The following Node.js code will add helmet's CSP middleware on each request so that the server responds with a CSP header and a simple security policy.

We define a whitelist where JavaScript code and CSS resources are only allowed to be loaded from the current origin, which is the exact hostname or domain (no sub-domains will be allowed):

---

[11]https://developer.mozilla.org/en-US/docs/Web/Security/CSP/CSP_policy_directives

Foreword

Node.js and JavaScript at large are quickly taking over software for the web. StackOverflow[1] and GitHub's[2] projects statistics strengthen this notion, showcasing JavaScript in the IoT industry, ChatOps projects, and general Enterprises adoption is growing as well for Node.js. With this trend in the rise for the past several years, it is imperative to take into account security practices and learn how to secure and harden Node.js Web Applications.

This book aims to equip existing Node.js developers with expertise and skills in security best practices. The book takes a practical hands-on approach to the Node.js ecosystem by using a good deal of source code examples, as well as leveraging and reviewing well tested and commonly used libraries and industry security standards.

---

[1] StackOverflow Developer Survey 2016: http://stackoverflow.com/research/developer-survey-2016
[2] GitHub Octoverse 2016: https://octoverse.github.com/

```
1  var helmet = require('helmet');
2
3  app.use(helmet.contentSecurityPolicy({
4    directives: {
5      scriptSrc: ["'self'"],
6      styleSrc: ["'self'"]
7    }
8  }));
```

It is important to remember that if no default policy is specified then all other types of content policies are open and allowed, and also some content policies simply don't have a default and must be specified to be overridden.

Let's construct the following content policy for our web application:

- By default, allow resources to be loaded only from our own domain origin, or from our Amazon CDN.
- JavaScript sources are restricted to our own domain and Google's hosted libraries domain so we can load AngularJS from Google.
- Because our web application doesn't need any kind of iframes, or objects to be embedded and rendered we will disable them.
- Forms are always only submitted to our own domain origin

```
1  var helmet = require('helmet');
2
3  app.use(helmet.contentSecurityPolicy({
4    directives: {
5      defaultSrc: ["'self'", 'https://cdn.amazon.com'],
6      scriptSrc: ["'self'", 'https://ajax.googleapis.com'],
7      childSrc: ["'none'"],
8      objectSrc: ["'none'"],
9      formAction: ["'none'"]
10   }
11 }));
```

Lusca Implementation

Lusca's CSP option has three main objects that can be set:

- `policy` - an object for defining the content policy

- `reportOnly` - a true or false for defining whether the browser should only report for violations of the content policy or actually deny such attempts
- `reportUri` - the URI string to send reporting data as JSON documents via POST requests being made from the browser

With this simple setup constructing a content policy is very similar to the official documentation with regards to directives and their values.

For example, let's setup the following content policy: * Allow by default content only from our own origin domain, and from https://ajax.googleapis.com * For any content violations just report the error, don't actually deny requests from being sent * For any content violations send a report to a remote system

```
var lusca = require('lusca');

app.use(lusca.csp({
  policy: {
    'default-src': "'self' https://ajax.googleapis.com"
  },
  reportOnly: true,
  reportUri: 'https://mydomain.com/report'
}));
```

Gradual CSP Implementation

Your Content Security Policy will grow and change as your web application grows too. With the wide and varied directives it could be challenging to introduce a policy all at once so instead a learning curve for what works is recommended.

The CSP header has a built-in directive which help in understanding how your web application makes use of content policy. This directive is used for reporting any actions performed by the browser for any of the directives and the origins that they call.

It's simple to add to any running web application:

```
Content-Security-Policy: default-src 'self'; report-uri https://mydomain.com/rep\
ort
```

Once added, the browser will send a POST request to the URI provided with a JSON format in the body for anything that violates the content security policy of serving content from our own origin domain where the page is served.

With Helmet this is easily configured:

```javascript
var helmet = require('helmet');

app.use(helmet.csp({
  directives: {
    defaultSrc: ['self'],
    reportUri: 'https://mydomain.com/report'
  }
}));
```

Another useful configuration for helmet when we are still evaluating is to instruct the browser to only report on content policy violation and not block them:

```javascript
var helmet = require('helmet');

app.use(helmet.csp({
  directives: {
    defaultSrc: ['self'],
    reportUri: 'https://mydomain.com/report'
  },
  reportOnly: true
}));
```

Other HTTP headers

Some other non-standard HTTP headers exist which are not part of any official specification such as IANA, but are worth looking into as they do provide another layer of security for your users.

X-XSS-Protection

The HTTP header *X-XSS-Protection* is used by IE8 and IE9, allows toggling on or off the Cross-Site-Scripting (XSS) filter capability that is built into the browser.

Turning XSS filtering for any IE8 and IE9 browsers on your web application requires to send the following HTTP header:

```
X-XSS-Protection: 1; mode=block
```

With Helmet, this protection can be turned on using the following snippet:

```
var helmet = require('helmet');

app.use(helmet.xssFilter());
```

With Lusca, this is quite simple as well:

```
var lusca = require('lusca');

app.use(lusca.xssProtection(true));
```

X-Content-Type-Options

The *X-Content-Type-Options* HTTP header is used by IE, Chrome, and Opera and is used to mitigate a MIME based attack.

The purpose of this header is mostly to instruct the browser to not sniff override the web server's content type and render the stream as is given from the server.

An example of setting this header:

```
X-Content-Type-Options: nosniff
```

Helmet's implementation:

```
var helmet = require('helmet');

app.use(helmet.noSniff());
```

Lusca has no support for this HTTP header built in.

Summary

In this chapter we dived into the world of security by implementing HTTP headers for increased security. We learned about Helmet, and Lusca Node.js libraries which can be easily added to any ExpressJS project and quickly configured to provide additional security.

The HTTP security headers that we reviewed are:

- Strict Transport Security
- X Frame Options
- Content Security Policy
- X XSS Protection
- X Content Type Options

Secure Session Management

If your web application is completely stateless and requires no user customization at all, and no user tracking then you probably don't even need to worry about users and sessions management.

The other scenario is that you need to serve content customized for users, allow them to login and perform some actions, or maintain a user related activity. This is where things get tricky and need proper attention to whole lot more details of information security.

HTTP being a stateless communication protocol, there-fore creating the need for a mechanism to track and maintain user's actions when interacting with a web applications - sessions.

The focus of this chapter will discuss Cookies based session management which is the most widespread way of maintaining sessions for web applications.

Session Security Risks

Improper session management in web applications may lead to several vulnerabilities that can be exploited by attackers.

 To understand session security in depth we first must own a basic understanding of sessions management. A web server keeps track of the user's browsing interaction by saving to the user's browser a token, often referred to as session id, which it uses to identify this unique user for further requests and interactions made between the user and the web server.

Reviewing a few examples of session related attacks:

- **Session Fixation** - by employing several vectors of attack, it attempts to gain a valid session on the browser, and then fixing the victim's browsing session to use the already existing session that attacker owns. Possible attack vectors are Cross-Site-Scripting (XSS), Meta Tag Injections, Session Adoption and others.
- **Session Hijacking** - an attacker will employ similar attack vectors such as XSS, and may also employ a MITM attack to reveal a valid user's session id so it can be hijacked by the attacker and made use of.

The risk and impact of any session attack is owning the user's identity and thus having the same privileged session as the user does. To compare with Unix attacks which may exploit root privilege escalation attacks, this introduces possibly the greatest risk for web applications as well.

On Session Management

OWASP maintains an up to date Session Management[12] checklist to validate your web security compliance with security standards.

Session Security in Node.js and ExpressJS

ExpressJS utilizes the express-session[13] middleware for session management. The project is well maintained, tested and de-facto solution for session management in Node.js.

Installing express-session:

```
npm install express-session --save
```

The following sections of this chapter will review how to safely configure a secured session management policy, building step-by-step on the available options of express-session.

The summary of this chapter will feature a complete session management configuration for your convenience.

Secure your traffic with HTTPs

Routing all of your HTTP traffic through a secured sockets layer such as SSL or TLS prevents attackers from sniffing your data on the wire and makes it harder for them to perform MITM attacks to eavesdrop your traffic.

Cookies may be set on the user browser with a flag to instruct the browser to only transmit cookies when working with HTTPS communication.

---

[12] https://www.owasp.org/index.php/Session_Management_Cheat_Sheet
[13] https://github.com/expressjs/session

```
1  var session = require('express-session');
2
3  app.use(session({
4    cookie: {
5      secure: true
6    }
7  }));
```

Secure cookie access to communication protocol only

Browsers feature a method for accessing client side cookie information through the common use of the document.cookie object. When a web application is made vulnerable to Cross-Site-Scripting (XSS) attacks then it can be exploited to run any arbitrary JavaScript code. Some examples are to access cookie information and perform any action on it, such as send it to a remote service controlled or monitored by the attacker, or just print it to the generated HTML page output.

To mitigate this issue, we can limit the access to the cookie information so that the browser knows to only send/receive cookie data via the HTTP/HTTPS communication protocol over the wire. Any attempts to execute JavaScript functions to get the cookie object will then fail.

```
1  var session = require('express-session');
2
3  app.use(session({
4    cookie: {
5      httpOnly: true
6    }
7  }));
```

Secure storage of session cookie

The session cookie is used to identify the user's browsing session at least, and may contain more sensitive information about the user and the web application in other cases. Due to the sensitive data that the cookie holds it's persistence and storage in the browser's client side makes it an appealing target for attackers and thus another very important aspect of security.

We identify two types of cookie storage: persistent and non-persistent cookies.

Persistent cookies are specified by a *Max-Age* or *Expires* attribute and value which define the amount of time to store on the browser's disk storage.

Non-persistent which are more secured will be stored in the browser's memory for the remainder of time when the browser process is open. Once closed, any cookie information that was saved in the browser is no longer available.

With express-session, the *maxAge* value is by default set to *null* which makes for a secure cookie configuration but it is worth forcing this value for clarity and for future updates to the library:

```
1  var session = require('express-session');
2
3  app.use(session({
4    cookie: {
5      // If required to set a persistent cookie to a specified time
6      // then use a maxAge value in milliseconds
7      maxAge: null;
8    }
9  }));
```

 Did you ever toggle the Remember Me option?
Web applications make use of persisting the cookie data to the user's disk storage in order to provide a more convenient user experience which doesn't require the user to always login. If the cookie is available on disk, the user's session remains active and can be continued from the point it was left off.

Obscuring the session identifier

The cookie name seems like a basic and unimportant piece of information as it's merely the name of the cookie but reality is far from basic.

Fingerprinting is an field in security which attempts to identify the services and their versions that power a service based on how they work and what they send. For example, a common PHP web application sets the cookie name to PHPSESSION, providing an attacker with a head-start of knowing already which platform is powering a web application, how and where to focus the vector of attack. In such cases, the attacker had already gathered information on the system without needing to do anything.

In Node.js case, ExpressJS's session middleware defaults to a cookie with a name of *connect.sid*. In attempt to hide this information from the outside world we can change the cookie name to anything else:

```
1  var session = require('express-session');
2
3  app.use(session({
4    name: 'CR7';
5  }));
```

Blackhatter?

If you ever wish to wear that black hat and explore other systems then you might want to use OWASP's Cookie Database[14] which is essentially a list of cookie names used by vendors, which will save you the trouble of fingerprinting this information on your own.

Secure session ID

When session IDs are the keys to identify users then their generation and randomness is of crucial importance. If they are generated in a way which allows to predict future values then they pose an immense risk as an attacker could attempt to brute force user sessions based on generating a predictable value until a hit is matched.

There are two aspects to session IDs: generating them, and signing them. With express-session we get access to influence both of those and can further secure our session identifiers.

Signing the session id with a long string provides more entropy. A good value will be at least 64 bits which gets added to the SHA-256 hashing of the cookie id being generated:

```
var session = require('session');

app.use(session({
  secret: 'THEWALL'
}));
```

Generating session ids is less likely to be altered from the default used by express-session which is the *uid-safe* library. If you do however require to override it with your own unique generator then it can be done by providing a function callback to the *genid* property.

```
var session = require('session');

app.use(session({
  genid: function(req) {
    return uniqueValue();
  }
}));
```

---

[14]https://www.owasp.org/index.php/Category:OWASP_Cookies_Database

Re-generating session IDs

The sensitive nature of the session identifier calls for more ways to protect it. A good defense against session fixation and also works well against session hijacking is to re-generate the session identifier. Doing this for every request might be an overkill, but it is quite common to do it before sensitive actions that are taken by the user and before any privilege escalation.

A good strategy for re-generating the session identifier is in all of the following cases:

- User login - after the user logged-in to the system, a new session identifier needs to be generated
- Sensitive actions, depending on the application but here is a reference:
    - Password change, email update and other personal details identifying the user
    - Assigning roles and permissions to other users
    - Deletion of records
    - Money transfer in banking applications, or buying stocks, and similar scenarios.

When using express-session, the middleware populates the `req.session` object with several methods and objects providing useful access to session management. One of those is `req.session.regenerate()` which is used for creating a new session identifier and is used as follows:

```
req.session.regenerate(function(err) {
  // new session identifier has been created
  // the req.session object has been re-instantiated with new values
});
```

Reference for secure session configuration

```
var session = require('express-session');

app.use(session({
  name: 'REPLACE_WITH_UNIQUE_NAME',
  secret: 'REPLACE_WITH_UNIQUE_SECRET',
  cookie: {
    maxAge: null,
    httpOnly: true,
    secure: true
  }
}));
```

Complete source code for a functional secure session-enabled server can be found in the book's GitHub repository.

Summary

In this chapter we learned essential session management best practices such as:

- Transmitting cookie information over HTTPS connections only
- Preventing access to cookie information from JavaScript runtime
- Obscuring the cookie name to hide your web application stack

```
app.get('/login', function(req, res, next) {
    // we send a dummy object for every request being made to /login path
    res.status(200).send({'login': 'ok'});
});
```

The *lookup* key passed to the *limits* object is very flexible and by default it will match any object/property options in ExpressJS request object. A short list of useful and informative request object properties are:

- headers.host
- headers.user-agent
- headers.accept-language
- headers.x-forwarded-for
- connection.remoteAddress and connection.remotePort
- url
- method
- path
- query
- protocol
- xhr
- ip

Usually other middlewares like *passport* which provide authentication and authorization capabilities extend the *req* object with more data such as the user information when logged in. Therefore another option to limit requests by is per the user id: *user.id*, or by username: *user.username*.

More information on how to limit requests based on other methods is available on express-limiter GitHub page[16].

Advanced Functionality Limiting

More tweaking can be performed to your web server layer to further close down on possible attack vectors. A library from Yahoo! allow for alerting these settings and is called limits[17], or *node-limits* if you would like to research it more on their GitHub page.

For example, if your web application has no notion of file uploads then you can disable completely these types of form submissions. If you do allow file uploads, you can limit the maximum size of a request that is sent to you for processing. These can help reduce any attempts to slow down

---

[16]https://github.com/ded/express-limiter
[17]https://github.com/yahoo/node-limits

your bandwidth and network pipeline and reduce temporary disk space or any operations that are performed by your web application to process file uploads.

Other tweaks this library provide is to configure timeout thresholds. For example, you may want to set a global timeout for incoming connections to make sure that an attacker does not attempt to keep many sockets opened on your web server OS.

Installing the *limits* library and updating the *package.json*:

```
npm install limits --save
```

Creating the following limit configuration:

- Disable file uploads
- Limit all requests to a total of 2 megabytes
- Set a global timeout for incoming connections to 1 minute

```
var nodeLimits = require('limits');

app.use(nodeLimits({
  file_uploads: false,
  post_max_size: 2000000,
  inc_req_timeout: 1000*60*60
}));
```

body-parser middleware

The body-parser[18] middleware augments ExpressJS web framework with support for requests being made and parsing the HTTP body data for common data types such as JSON. *body-parser* is quite popular and is reported to serve more than five million downloads a month.

npm v1.15.2 | downloads 76M | build passing | coverage 100%

As seen with the previous *limits* library, it is possible to limit the incoming request size so it doesn't cause server CPU strain to parse the body object. Where the *limits* library may be an overkill for some web applications, *body-parser* is quite common and can be set to limit the specific requests it handles to provide security.

To install and update the *package.json* file with the *body-parser* library:

---
[18]https://github.com/expressjs/body-parser

```
npm install body-parser --save
```

Limiting request sizes works as follows:

```
var bodyParser = require('body-parser');

// instruct bodyParser to parse JSON data and populate the body data payload
// in the request object *req* with an actual JSON object
app.use(bodyParser.json({
  limit: '1mb'
}));
```

Once the limit has been set, when an incoming request is bigger than the limit then ExpressJS will emit the error *request entity too large* which is a standard HTTP response and reply with a 413 HTTP code.

enforcing limits

Remember that *body-parser* only handles non-multipart form submissions so setting this limit will not affect file uploads being sent to your web application.

Summary

In this chapter we reviewed some tools and configurations that aid in hardening an ExpressJS web application, such as implementing rate limiting to mitigate flood of requests, implmenting quota for file uploads and generally hiding the details of ExpressJS as the application framework.

The ExpressJS documentation also provides further details and insights with regards to security best practices that help harden and secure ExpressJS applications. Product Best Practices[19] review some of this information and will most probably receive updates in the future so this is always a good resource to keep track on.

---

[19] http://expressjs.com/en/advanced/best-practice-security.html

Cross-Site Request Forgery (CSRF)

Named after the attack it employs, a CSRF tricks the victim to unknowingly send requests to a system where the user has access to, and is presumably already logged-in to. Usually these attacks are targeted by nature as the attacker would have to craft a CSRF and trick the user into performing an action on another system than that of the attacker. Thus, the attacker probably has previous knowledge of the target system for which the CSRF is crafted.

Known by other names

CSRF has a bunch of other names which other vendors and communities use, namely: One-Click attack by Microsoft, Session Riding, and is often even abbreviated as XSRF.

The Risk

An example use case is where a vulnerable web application might have a form which makes use of the GET method to be submitted and so it receives its input field data from the query parameters. In this case, a user can be easily tricked into submitting that GET method HTML FORM through several ways:

- A fake e-mail or website, attracting the user to click on a link or even just try to render an image that will lead to submitting this form. For example:

```
<img src="http://target-web-application.com/updateEmailAddress.php?email=attacke\
r@domain.com" />
```

When the user's email client will attempt to interpret this HTML piece and render the image tag then it will actually cause the browser to make that request on behalf of the user. If the user is logged-in then this example GET method FORM will be submitted, resulting in the user's email address to be changed.

- A naive-looking link can also lead the user to click on it without the user's knowledge of what this link action actually calls to:

```
1  <a href="http://target-web-application.com/updateEmailAddress.php?email=attacker\
2  @domain.com"> Read More </a>
```

Updating the form implementation to use POST or PUT requests doesn't provide any higher level of security for implementing secure forms. Some examples for attacking these forms are:

- The attacker controls a website which can contain a naive-looking form submission with the action path set to the targeted vulnerable web application. For example:

```
1  <form action="http://target-web-application.com/updateEmailAddress.php" method="\
2  post">
3  <input type="hidden" name="email" value="attacker@domain.com" />
4  <input type="submit" value="Continue" />
5  </form>
```

When clicked, the browser will send a request to the path specified in the *action* property with a hidden key/value pair of updating the user's email address.

- An attacker can also leverage JavaScript code to submit the former POST method FORM example with the page load event so the user has nothing to say about it (except if the user has JavaScript disabled):

```
1  <body onLoad="document.forms[0].submit()">
```

- Another case which can be exploited by the user is to create an AJAX request which trigger the browser to process and send this request:

```
1  <script type="text/javascript">
2  var xhr = new XMLHttpRequest();
3  xhr.open("POST", "http://target-web-application.com/updateEmailAddress.php");
4  xhr.setRequestHeader("Content-Type", "application/x-www-form-urlencoded");
5  xhr.send("email=attacker@domain.com");
6  </script>
```

This AJAX request can also run automatically when the user loads the attacker's web page with simply binding it to the *onLoad* event.

An even greater risk is where the target web application is actually hosting the CSRF code. For example, if the web application allows rich text comments, forums, or any other rich user input then it makes a very appealing target for attackers to inject a CSRF attck there and greatly increase this vulnerability.

The Solution

As described when reviewing the possible risks of CSRF, any attempts to attempt and harden an HTML FORM entity are futile and are mere annoyance for an attacker to workaround, but such attempts are definitely not the solution.

To be clear, let's review what would be a wrong way of approaching a CSRF solution:

1. Changing the FORM *method* attribute from GET to POST
2. Changing the FORM *action* attribute value from HTTP to HTTPS endpoint, or updating the URI to a full URL.
3. Deprecating all the FORM elements and converting them to API endpoint
4. Adding further actions to confirm the FORM submission such as popups or secondary forms
5. Storing any hidden information inside a Cookie to authorize requests

All of the above are examples of what not to do in order to protect against CSRF vulnerabilities, because some are either wrong, give an illusion of a solution, or simply do not fix the problem entirely.

CSRF Tokens

The preferred way to protect against CSRF attacks is by generating a token, which is in essence a random, unguessable string, for every action that is performed by the user. With every user's action this token is then being compared between what the user sent and what the server expects (the previous token that was generated). In cases where the comparison fails the CSRF tokens mis-match and the action is being denied as well due to a potential attack.

CSRF tokens can be further secured by not using a single token for the entire user session, which might be common with Single Page Application architecture (SPA), but rather new tokens can be generated and compared with for every form action submitted or similar user action being taken.

 Unreadable characters we call CAPTCHAs
The concept of CAPTCHAs was initially introduced to mitigate user spam, bots, and automated web crwaling. It is a possible solution to add security for forms and actions but it is not user friendly. By the way, did you know that the meaning of CAPTCHA is: Completely Automated Public Turing Test To Tell Computers and Humans Apart. Luckily we have an acronym for it.

CSRF Tokens Implementation

There are several ways to implement the CSRF Token and they vary and depend on a web application's architecture. The fundamentals of comparing a generated token with the one received in the input remains the same, only the delivering and exchanging the token between the server and the client changes.

Request Body

With the Request Body implementation, the server generates the CSRF token which is then being used in the view layer to be placed on the forms to be submitted as a hidden input element. When the user submits the form, the hidden input element with the CSRF value is also sent as part of the request body, which is then received by the server and the server can compare the CSRF token from the input to the token that was generated with the page view.

This approach requires per page handling of the CSRF token so it must be pre-planned and designed when creating the web page, hence making it cumbersome from application architecture perspective. Moreover, with Single Page Applications (SPA) the architecture dictates a single page load, so the server is actually generating the CSRF token only one time, and that token needs to be compared with every subsequent requests being sent by the web application.

CSRF Cookie

Most web applications require to utilize cookies for client-side storage and maintaining a session in a stateless HTTP protocol. By leveraging the cookie store, the web application can set a CSRF cookie with the token's value. At this point all the cookies for the web application will be sent with every request the user makes to the server, including the previously set CSRF token cookie. This by itself adds no protection, but implementing what is known as a Double Submit Cookies mechanism will do the job. Double Submit Cookies works by sending random values in both the request query itself as well as a cookie value, which then the server compares and confirms.

CSRF Token Header

Relying on a custom HTTP header to exchange information about the CSRF token is considered a high level of security, since it requires from an attacker to actually be able to "sniff" the network traffic or perform a Man-In-The-Middle (MITM) attack.

In cases where both the server and the client utilize the specific CSRF Token Header then when the server generates the token it responds with this special token, and when the client receives the response it can parse the HTTP header for the token value, and then sends it back to the server as the same HTTP header which the server expects.

CSRF Libraries - under the hood

Inspecting the source code of csurf[20] library provides more insight on the internals of how a CSRF library handles the token and where it expects it, with the order of precedence:

```
/**
 * Default value function, checking the `req.body`
 * and `req.query` for the CSRF token.
 *
 * @param {IncomingMessage} req
 * @return {String}
 * @api private
 */

function defaultValue(req) {
  return (req.body && req.body._csrf)
    || (req.query && req.query._csrf)
    || (req.headers['csrf-token'])
    || (req.headers['xsrf-token'])
    || (req.headers['x-csrf-token'])
    || (req.headers['x-xsrf-token']);
}
```

If a token comparison failed, the csurf library will thrown an error[21]:

```
/**
 * Verify the token.
 *
 * @param {IncomingMessage} req
 * @param {Object} tokens
 * @param {string} secret
 * @param {string} val
 * @api private
 */

function verifytoken(req, tokens, secret, val) {
  // valid token
  if (!tokens.verify(secret, val)) {
    throw createError(403, 'invalid csrf token', {
      code: 'EBADCSRFTOKEN'
```

---

[20] https://github.com/expressjs/csurf/blob/master/index.js#L115
[21] https://github.com/expressjs/csurf/blob/master/index.js#L115

```
16      });
17    }
18  }
```

To summarize, the server which implements the *csurf* library will always look for the CSRF token in either the request parameters, the body payload or in a specific HTTP header. It takes this value and compares it with the value it stored initially to check for a match.

ExpressJS csurf Library

csurf[22] is another middleware from the ExpressJS family, which provides a mechanism to manage CSRF tokens.

The *csurf* library makes use of either the server's session storage or the client's cookie storage to persist and compare the CSRF token, therefore it must be used together with either of them. This chapter will cover usage with both of these options.

Installing *csurf* for use in an expressjs project:

```
1  npm install csurf --save
```

csurf With Cookies

The minimal requirement for *csurf* is the body-parser[23] library to access the data from the *req* object, and then either the session library *express-session*), or the cookie-parser[24] library to persist the CSRF token value.

To begin, all the libraries are required in the code:

```
1  var bodyParser = require('body-parser');
2  var cookieParser = require('cookie-parser');
3  var csrf = require('csurf');
```

Next, the libraries are initialized and configured:

---

[22] https://github.com/expressjs/csurf
[23] https://github.com/expressjs/body-parser
[24] https://www.npmjs.com/package/cookie-parser

```
// initialize the body-parser library
app.use(bodyParser.urlencoded());

// setup cookie information
app.use(cookieParser('secretKey'));
```

Only then, the csurf middleware can be initialized (this order of middlewares is important). csurf is configured to use the cookies storage and is added as part of the middleware for an ExpressJS *app* object:

```
var csrfToken = csrf({cookie: true});
app.use(csrfToken);
```

From this point on, all is left is to configure the route to have access to the CSRF token. By using a simple example where a view renders an HTML FORM element, the route provides the CSRF token to the hidden CSRF token input field.

```
app.get('/login', function(req, res, next) {
  res.render('login', {
    csrfToken: req.csrfToken()
  })
});
```

The view for the */login* route is a simple FORM that uses the *csrfToken* variable in the template as part of a hidden input field:

```
<form action="/login" method="post">
<input type="hidden" name="_csrf" value="<%= csrfToken %>">
<button type="submit">Submit</button>
</form>
```

The view references the */login* path when submitted and sends this as a POST HTTP request. The example route added below to handle the form submission will only meet and return an HTTP 200 response if the CSRF token passed validation:

```
app.post('/login', function(req, res, next) {
  res.status(200).send({
    'csrf': 'ok'
  });
});
```

csurf With Session

The following libraries are first required in the code:

```
var bodyParser = require('body-parser');
var session = require('express-session');
var csrf = require('csurf');
```

Because we are using sessions for persistence, the session ideally needs to be configured, and we also initialize the body-parser library so that csurf middleware can locate the required token in the *req* object:

```
// configure session and cookie details
app.use(session({
  name: 'csrfExampleSession',
  secret: 'csrfSecretExampleKey',
  resave: true,
  saveUninitialized: true,
  cookie: {
    maxAge: null,
    httpOnly: true,
    secure: false
  }
}));

// initialize the body-parser library
app.use(bodyParser.urlencoded());
```

From this point on, the flow is similar to how the csrf with cookies configuration works. All is left is to configure the route to have access to the CSRF token. By using a simple example where a view renders an HTML FORM element, the route provides the CSRF token to the hidden CSRF token input field.

```
1  app.get('/login', function(req, res, next) {
2    res.render('login', {
3      csrfToken: req.csrfToken()
4    })
5  });
```

The view for the */login* route is a simple FORM that uses the *csrfToken* variable in the template as part of a hidden input field:

```
1  <form action="/login" method="post">
2    <input type="hidden" name="_csrf" value="<%= csrfToken %>">
3    <button type="submit">Submit</button>
4  </form>
```

The view references the */login* path when submitted and sends this as a POST HTTP request. The example route added below to handle the form submission will only meet and return an HTTP 200 response if the CSRF token passed validation:

```
1  app.post('/login', function(req, res, next) {
2    res.status(200).send({
3      'csrf': 'ok'
4    });
5  });
```

ExpressJS With lusca Library

lusca[25] is a web application security middleware, which amongst many other features that were covered in earlier chapters, also provide CSRF Token security and integrates with web application frameworks such as ExpressJS.

`npm v1.4.1` `build passing`

Similar to csurf[26], *lusca* also requires either a session or cookie middleware for storage and persistence, as well as the *body-parser* middleware.

Installing lusca if this hasn't been done in previous chapters:

---

[25]https://github.com/krakenjs/lusca
[26]https://github.com/expressjs/csurf

```
1  npm install lusca --save
```

lusca With Session

The application setup is very similar to that of *csurf* so it is provided here as a full source code example and the *csurf* sections can be referred to for specific references of each chunk of code.

```
1   var express = require('express');
2   var session = require('express-session');
3   var bodyParser = require('body-parser');
4   var lusca = require('lusca');
5
6   // configure session and cookie details
7   app.use(session({
8     name: 'luscaCsrfExampleSession',
9     secret: 'luscaCsrfSecretExampleKey',
10    resave: true,
11    saveUninitialized: true,
12    cookie: {
13      maxAge: null,
14      httpOnly: true,
15      secure: false
16    }
17  }));
18
19  app.use(bodyParser.urlencoded());
20
21  var luscaCsrf = lusca({csrf: true});
22  app.use(luscaCsrf);
23
24  app.get('/login', function(req, res, next) {
25    res.render('login', {
26      csrfToken: req.csrfToken()
27    })
28  });
29
30  app.post('/login', function(req, res, next) {
31    res.status(200).send({
32      'csrf': 'ok'
33    });
34  });
```

Summary

Implementing CSRF token security to mitigate CSRF attacks is a vital and fundamental layer to secure a web application client-side user.

While we reviewed *csurf* and *lusca* as viable libraries to integrate into a working Node.js application, there are other implementations both client-side and server-side to help protect end-users. One example is AngularJS's built-in support for CSRF token mechanism that can be further consulted in their $http service documentation[27].

---

[27] https://docs.angularjs.org/api/ng/service/\protect\char"0024\relaxhttp

Cross-Site Scripting (XSS)

A Cross-Site Scripting (XSS) attack is characterized by an attacker's ability to inject to a web application, scripts of any kind, such as Flash, HTML, or JavaScript, that are intended to run and render on the application serving the page. The web application unintentionally serves the script code which is executed by the browser and hence makes the user vulnerable to data theft and any privileges level which the script is allowed.

The source of an XSS vulnerability lies in a web application that allows malicious code to be injected and evaluated as part of the web page being served to the user, and then the same malicious code is executed by the browser due to the web application inability to filter and sanitize the output.

To explore an example of a simple use case - A web page which reads the user's name from the query parameter http://example.com/profile?name=John, and then it uses this parameter to display the user's name on a profile page:

```
<div>
  <h2>{{name}}</h2>
</div>
```

What would happen if someone were to replace the string *John* with JavaScript code?

```
http://example.com/profile?name=<script>alert("xss")</script>
```

If no string escaping is performed on the *name* parameter at the output level, or at least some sanitization on the data that is expected for the *name* parameter to be valid, then the rendered page will actually have the JavaScript code printed out to the user and the browser which renders this script will display an alert dialog box:

```
<div>
  <h2><script>alert("xss")</script></h2>
</div>
```

The Risk

XSS vulnerabilities can be classified in one of the following categories:

- Stored/Persistent XSS - As it name implies, a stored XSS attack is when the malicious XSS code is injected to the web application and is stored on the persistent storage which the application implements. For example, if the web application would allow comments, and the comments input is not validated or sanitized then an attacker could inject malicious XSS code as part of the comment. Due to the comment being stored in the web application, when the page renders the comment view for any user it will also expose the user to this attack.
- Reflected XSS - This type of XSS attack has the same result for the end user, but is less severe from a stored XSS because the web application is not exposing all users alike to the malicious code but instead, an attacker is able to craft a malicious link that when the user is tricked into viewing it then the request injects the malicious code into the web application and then renders on the user's browser.

    For example, imagine a search query being made: http://example.com/search?movieName=Inception where a common web application will make use of the *movieName* parameter to inform the user what he searched for. If the web application is insecure a reflected XSS attack can occur with an attacker being able to replace the value for the *movieName* parameter with a malicious JavaScript executable code.
- DOM-based XSS - The nature of this XSS attack lies in the web application code making use of DOM methods which rely on insecure user input. Browsers provide the most commonly used *document* object which allows to interact with the web page structure and the current web request that was made. Vulnerable properties of the *document* object are *document.location* or *document.documentURI* to name a few. If a web application uses one of these properties insecurely to parse data from the request being made and then use it in the web page then an attacker is able to alter the request just like with a reflected XSS attack and thus affect the DOM structure and expose the user's browser to execute the malicious code.

Briefly reviewing the sources of untrusted input data which may be vulnerable to XSS attacks:

- Query string and parameters - these are the most common input injections and include any *GET* parameters, the URL itself or pieces of it, and general *POST* data or other HTML methods.
- Cookies - even cookies may contain data which an attacker was able to somehow inject malicious code into and should be treated with care.

Variations of XSS syntax

JavaScript being the most widely used language for malicious code, it can be represented and transmitted in ways other than the common `<script>` tags.

For example, XSS using HTML event attributes. HTML supports DOM events to be assigned as an attribute to HTML entities. When assigned, the events allow to execute JavaScript code which doesn't need to be wrapped inside `<script>` ... `</script>` tags:

```
1   <button onClick="alert('xss')">Submit</button>
```

The risk presented with this attack is that web applications that attempt to blacklist or filter so-called risky HTML tags like the script tags will fail in this case where the attacker is able to inject JavaScript code to the page by including it as part of the allowed DOM events.

More resources to get acquainted with XSS related injection:

- **XSS syntax variations** - OWASP Wiki includes a comprehensive and very detailed XSS Filter Evasion Cheat Sheet[28] which features the many variations of possible injections that can be employed by an attacker to bypass your protection controls and succeed with an XSS attack.
- **HTML5 Security** - Due to the new HTML5 specification, browsers are adopting new directives, attributes, elements and this introduces new vectors of attack, some of which are related to XSS. html5sec[29] is a good reference website to keep up to date with such vulnerabilities related to insecure adoption of HTML5 features.

The Solution

XSS vulnerabilities expose and attack the end user by exploiting browser execution of unintentional injected code into the page. As such, the path for defending against XSS attacks lies on the client side when outputting potentially dangerous user data input.

There are two primary methods to prevent XSS attacks:

- **Filtering** - by filtering, or sanitizing the untrusted data that originated from the user's input the end result is that the data is modified and removed of the original text that it contained. If for example a user on a blog wanted to comment and give an example of the use of `<script>` tags then filtering based on a blacklist/whitelist will remove any offending tags such as `<script>`, even if the user did not intend to execute this code on the browser maliciously but rather just to print it and share the text on the website.

Pitfalls of filtering is that it relies on a blacklist or a whitelist which could be subject to frequent changes, hence it requires maintenance and error-prone, and it usually requires complex string manipulation logic that is often based on regular expressions which by themselves can become a security threat or simply not being written correctly to address future changes and string alterations that the programmer did not expect thus could be bypassed.

---

[28] https://www.owasp.org/index.php/XSS_Filter_Evasion_Cheat_Sheet
[29] https://html5sec.org/

- **Escaping/Encoding** - Unlike filtering, encoding the untrusted data preserves all the input which the user supplied by escaping potentially malicious characters with their display character encoding. For example, if the input from the user is expected to be an HTML text and it is also treated as such, then in cases where the input is `<script>alert('xss')</script>` then it is possible to encode the `<` symbol to its HTML entity representation which is `&lt;`. This character entity has also a number associated with, so the `<` symbol could also be represented with the string `&#60;` which will result in the same encoding behavior. Browsers know how to parse these entities and display them correctly.

The important nuance of encoding data is to encode it with the correct context of where it will be used. JSON, HTML, and CSS are all different in their encoding and one does not match the other so based on where the input is planned to be utilized the correct form of encoding should be used.

In summary, filtering is not the ideal solution to prevent XSS attacks. Validation and filtering of the data should happen on the user's data input and not on the output processing. Encoding the outputted data is on the other hand a better path to take to prevent XSS attacks as it renders any data as plain text which the browser won't be tricked into executing.

XSS attacks evolve

Specifications, browsers, and the web in it's entirety constantly changes and introduces new technologies that web applications adopt and security needs to be adopted for as well. As such, XSS attacks have a great variety of attack vectors to exploit and increasingly harder to defend from and patch.

Encoding libraries: node-esapi

OWASP has their own ESAPI[30] project which aims to provide security relates tools, libraries and APIs that developers can adopt in order to provide essential security. This project has been ported to a Node.js library that is available as an npm package and is called *node-esapi*.

node-esapi[31] can be installed as any other npm package, and also update the *package.json* file with its dependency:

```
npm install node-esapi --save
```

Once installed, the library provides encoding functions for each type of data that should be encoded, so that the following general guideline should be applied:

---

[30] https://www.owasp.org/index.php/ESAPI
[31] https://github.com/ESAPI/node-esapi

Hardening ExpressJS

While ExpressJS is a very popular, and mature library for a web application framework it still can be tuned beyond the default options that it uses and those that are used by its related middleware plugins. ExpressJS is trusted by many users to run in production sites, and an extra attention to details and how to augment it are crucial in ensuring you have a security-hardened setup.

Security Through Obscurity

ExpressJS follows standards for HTTP web servers and as such it will send by default the *X-Powered-By* header which reports to any web request which web server is processing the request. Such information disclosure for attackers is welcomed with open arms as they have gained knowledge on which framework you are using and can focus their request to speer attacks specific to ExpressJS.

One of the first, very basic and easy hardening action web applications can take is to remove this header:

```
1  var express = require('express');
2  var app = express();
3
4  app.disable('x-powered-by');
```

Brute-Force Protection

Brute-force attacks may be employed by an attacker to send a series of username/password pairs to your REST end-points over POST or another RESTful API that you have opened to implement them. Such a dictionary attack is very straight-forward and easy to execute and may be performed on any other parts of your API or page routing, unrelated to logins.

A popular use-case is where you may have an administrative interface at the */admin* route and an attacker may try to issue automated requests there with different tokens, different cookie identifier etc to try and get in.

To help mitigate and limit requests being made to your web application we can leverage a library called express-limiter[15] which provides a very flexible configuration to integrate into an ExpressJS application.

---

[15] https://github.com/ded/express-limiter

Pre-requisite

A pre-requisite for using *express-limiter* is that it requires a Redis datastore to connect to and manage the limits it imposes per request.

Installing *express-limiter* and updating our *package.json* file with its entry:

```
npm install express-limiter --save
```

Let's create the following limit:

- Limit all type of requests (GET, POST, PUT, etc) to the */login* path
- Limit the requests based on the incoming IP address
- Allow a total of 20 requests per hour

```
var express = require('express');
var limiter = require('express-limiter');

// create a redisClient object with default connection information
var redisClient = require('redis').createClient();

// instantiate an express's app variable
var app = express();

// bind the limiter object the express app object and pass the redisClient
// object so it knows how to persist the imposed limits
var limits = limiter(app, redisClient);

/**
 * Configuring the following limits:
 * - Limit all type of requests (GET, POST, PUT, etc) to the /login path
 * - Limit the requests based on the incoming IP address
 * - Allow a total of 20 requests per hour
 */
limits({
  path: '/login',
  method: 'all',
  lookup: ['connection.remoteAddress'],
  total: 20,
  expire: 1000*60*60
});
```

- Use JavaScript encoding when untrusted input data is to be placed within the context of an executable JavaScript code. For example, a string of input from the user is expected to be used in a JavaScript source code such as `<script>showErrorMessage(userInput)</script>`.
- Use HTML encoding when untrusted input data is to placed within HTML markup. For example if the data is to be placed inside `<div>` tags, `<span>` tags, etc.

To encode HTML:

```
var esapi = require('node-esapi');
var esapiEncoder = esapi.encoder();

app.get('/', function(req, res, next) {

  // example for unsafe user input intended for embedding in HTML markup
  // req.query.userinput may include the string:
  // <div><span>Example</span><script>alert('xss')</script></div>
  var userInputExample = req.query.userinput;

  // encodedInput is now safe to output in an HTML context of the web page
  var encodedInput = esapiEncoder.encodeForHTML(userInputExample);
});
```

 Encoding for other data representations.
node-esapi also includes encoders for CSS, URL, HTML Attributes, and for Base64 representation of data.

Encoding libraries: xss-filters

From the home of Yahoo!, xss-filters[32] is another XSS encoding library. It is designed to follow HTML5 specification for implementation of XSS filters, and is constantly reviewed by security researchers from Yahoo!.

It is important to notice that *xss-filters* are intended to be used only inside an HTML markup context. You should not use it for any untrusted user input in other contexts like JavaScript or CSS code, or other specific objects like `<svg>`, `<object>`, or `<embed>` tags.

---

[32] https://github.com/yahoo/xss-filters

🔑 Yahoo! is quite active in the Node.js community

Did you know that Yahoo! is an active player in the Node.js community? They have contributed to the npm repository about a hundred of packages altogether with general JavaScript, and frontend libraries, amongst Node.js.

Installing *xss-filters*:

```
npm install xss-filters --save
```

Using the library to encode:

```javascript
var xssFilters = require('xss-filters');

app.get('/', function(req, res, next) {
  var userInput = req.query.userinput;
  var safeUserInput = xssFilters.inHTMLData(userInput);

  // do something with safeUserInput that is now encoded and safe to print
  // out in an HTML context
});
```

Besides *inHTMLData* there are other APIs that exist to handle encoding untrusted data in other context:

- HTML comments *inHTMLComment* - to encode data in HTML comment's such as `<!-- {{comment}} -->`
- HTML attributes - to encode data in HTML attributes it is required to make use of the appropriate quoting notation used in the attributes context.

With regards to HTML attributes, when using a single quote notation in attributes then use the *inSingleQuoteAttr* method:

JavaScript:

```javascript
var safeUserInput = xssFilters.inSingleQuotedAttr(userInput);
```

HTML:

```
1  <input value='{{safeUserInput}}'/>
```

When using double quotes notation in attributes then use the *inDoubleQuotedAttr* method:

JavaScript:

```
1  var safeUserInput = xssFilters.inDoubleQuotedAttr(userInput);
```

HTML:

```
1  <input value="{{safeUserInput}}"/>
```

When not using any type quotation as attributes in HTML elements, for example to specify attribute keywords `hidden` which is applied to an HTML element and makes it invisible then use the *inUnQuotedAttr* method:

JavaScript:

```
1  var safeUserInput = xssFilters.inUnQuotedAttr(userInput);
```

HTML:

```
1  <input name="csrfToken" value="{{csrfValue}}" {{safeUserInput}}/>
```

To further fine-tune the context of the untrusted input from the user, such as whether it is originated from a URI input then it is possible to use a specific method such as:

```
1  var userURIInput = xssFilters.uriInHTMLData();
2  var userURIPathInput = xssFilters.uriPathInHTMLData();
3  var userURIGragmentInput = xssFilters.uriFragmentInHTMLData();
```

Summary

OWASP ranks Cross Site Scripting (XSS) in the 3rd position of the Top 10 vulnerabilities and attack vectors[33]. As such, our awareness of security concerns should be high for attacks which are very common and easy to exploit.

To prevent XSS vulnerabilities, we learned about one of the basic mitigation techniques which is to encode or escape the output data so that malicious user input would not compromise the user's web browser by interpreting a maliciously injected JavaScript code.

The libraries we reviewed to mitigate XSS are OWASP's own node-esapi and Yahoo!'s xss-filters.

---

[33] https://www.owasp.org/index.php/Top10#OWASP_Top_10_for_2013

Secure Code Guidelines

Secure code guidelines are best practices which are set by organization, individuals, or anyone else to provide a set of standards or rules to follow that enable a person to write secure code. They are different for every programming language, and different guidelines may be set for the same language or platform by different organizations. Adopting a secure code guideline which is in-par with your requirements and company culture ensures quality software, and enhances awareness for security in the team.

Enforcing Secure Code Guidelines

To further strengthen the adoption in your team it is possible to create linting rules and git hooks that ensures source code that is being added to the source code repository is actually following the standards set for a secure code guideline. OWASP maintains a secure code guideline document[34] as a reference.

The Risk

These days attackers aim at application layers as they attempt to exploit vulnerable application code which isn't handling input correctly. Untrusted user input is the first line of defense for an application program code, and mitigating it early in the software development life-cycle is crucial in setting the security boundaries correctly and the foundations for a secure application design.

Failure of securely handling untrusted user input may result in:

- Injection attacks
- Information Disclosure
- Buffer Overflows leading to system compromise or memory leaks

Input Validation

A program performs input validation to ensure that the received data structure is valid, and as-expected for further handling and manipulation. Untrusted data, such as that which is originating from user input, may contain malicious or invalid data which can lead the program to perform unwanted tasks or cause side-effects.

Due to JavaScript's loosely typed nature, it is required to follow input validation in particular order for safety:

---

[34] https://www.owasp.org/index.php/OWASP_Secure_Coding_Practices_-_Quick_Reference_Guide

1. Existence - Whether the input data exists.
2. Length - When length matters, check that input data is constraint to a specific length or expected size.
3. Type - Confirming that a received user data matches an expected type. Ideally, where strict type checking is possible, such as with TypeScript[35], this is the preferred method. Otherwise, either basic language types or when expecting all numerics, or all characters, it is best to at least match the expected data.
4. Range - Where the range of values is constraint by your application logic, it is best to confirm that received data indeed matches the range.
5. Blacklisting and Whitelisting - Blacklisting is often less advised due to the fact that it is based on a perceived knowledge of vulnerabilities that the user expects, yet often times it is circumvented using new attacks. Whitelisting is advised as it matches only an expected user input.

 Node.js regular expressions are a big no-no due to the horrible ReDoS attacks that can bring down a server. With Node.js being single threaded in nature this becomes super critical and must be carefully observed.

Often, programmers tend to write their own Regular Expressions to validate input, for example, testing whether a received data input matches an e-mail address, a URL address and so on. While regex seem like an easy and natural solution for validating input, if not done correctly, they can be abused using attack vectors like ReDoS.

The ideal solution for validating user input is to use one of the following libraries which are constantly tested for security:

- npm's Validator - provides validation and sanitization capabilities
- OWASP's EASPIJS - OWASP's own implementation of that provides both input validation as well as output encoding capabilities.

Using Validator.js

Validator.js[36] is a well tested JavaScript library, that can be utilized both in the server-side as well as the client-side, for validating string data.

Validating e-mail addresses:

---

[35] https://www.typescriptlang.org
[36] https://github.com/chriso/validator.js

```
1  var validator = require('validator');
2  var isValidEmail = validator.isEmail('foo@bar.com');
```

Output Encoding

Output Encoding is a mechanism that is used at the presentation layer, where data that is passed from the server-side to a view, such as a web browser, which should be encoded or sanitized from malicious payloads which seek to exploit vulnerabilities in the presentation layer engine.

Implementing output encoding mitigates attacks such as Cross Site Scripting (XSS) because such malicious data is being encoded when it is output by the application to the presentation layer, hence circumventing any attempt to trick, or trigger an incorrect execution that is not a simple string representation of the data.

Terminology

Output Encoding is often referred to as Output Escaping, Output Handling. Often times another term is associated with output encoding - Canonicalization, which means to convert the untrusted data input into an expected representation in the correct context. For example, a given user input of `<script>alert()</script>` will be canonicalized to `&lt;script&gt;alert();&lt;/script&gt;`

Context is the most important thing about getting output encoding right. It is crucial to apply the type of encoding data for output based on the correct context of the presentation layer. When output is used in an HTML context, the encoding needs to apply HTML entities encoding, where-as when the output is used in a JavaScript context, then another type of encoding needs to happen to properly escape JavaScript code so it is not executed. Other output contexts to name a few are URLs, SQL, or system command calls.

Using ESAPI for Output Encoding

Node ESAPI[37] is OWASP's Enterprise Security API ported to Node.js.

The Node ESAPI project provides the functionality of encoding output for proper contexts, and it features both a functional way of using it like other npm packages, as well as integration with ExpressJS middleware layer.

Encoding output in the context of HTML:

---

[37] https://github.com/ESAPI/node-esapi

```
1  var esapi = require('node-esapi');
2  var esapiEncoder = esapi.encoder();
3
4  var htmlOutput = esapiEncoder.encodeForHTML('<div> Hello World! <script type="ja\
5  vascript"> alert("Got you!") </script> </div>');
```

The result of `htmlOutput` will be properly encoded to escape the malicious script tags:

```
1  &lt;div&gt; Hello World&#x21; &lt;script type&#x3d;&quot;javascript&quot;&gt; al\
2  ert&#x28;&quot;Got you&#x21;&quot;&#x29; &lt;&#x2f;script&gt; &lt;&#x2f;div&gt;
```

ESAPI provides the functionality for the following output encoding contexts:

- HTML - encodeForHTML
- CSS - encodeForCSS
- JavaScript - encodeForJS
- URL - encodeForURL
- HTML Attributes - encodeForHTMLAttribute
- Base64 - encodeForBase64

Output Encoding Libraries

Except from OWASP's ESAPI project there are other libraries that can be utilized for output encoding in Node.js server-side. As we learned about encoding, it is very important to use libraries to encode their dedicated context only. For example, using the encode-html library to only encode HTML-context text, and nothing else (not JavaScript, or CSS).

HTML Encoding

escape-html[38] is a very popular and mature library that can be used on the server-side coupled with template engines or views in order to safely encode HTML output sent to the browser.

After installing the library, it only exports a single function and that is `escape`.

```
1  var escape = require('escape-html');
2  var encodedHTML = escape('<p style="color: red;"> Hello World! <p>');
```

The `encodedHTML` value will be a valid encoded HTML entities:

---

[38] https://www.npmjs.com/package/escape-html

```
1  &lt;p style=&quot;color: red;&quot;&gt; Hello World! &lt;/p&gt;
```

CSS Encoding

cssesc[39] is a library that serves both Node.JS and the browsers for escaping and optimizing CSS outupt. It has a slimmed down version specifically for Node.JS that is called CSS.escape[40].

To install both of them (not actually required):

```
1  npm install cssesc
```

cssesc API exposes a function that takes an input value to escape and a second argument for specifying options.

```
1  var cssesc = require('cssesc');
2  var encodedCSS = cssesc('Node.js security © 2016');
```

The special copyright character will be encoded properly to be used in a valid CSS file:

```
1  Node.js security \A9  2016
```

JavaScript Encoding

js-string-escape[41] is another popular library which is used to encode text for a JavaScript specific context.

```
1  var jsescape = require('js-string-escape');
2  var encodedJS = jsescape('alert("test")');
```

A valid JavaScript encoded version of the alert text will be properly escaped as seen below. It isn't however JSON-compliant as can be seen:

```
1  alert(\"test\")
```

Regular Expressions

The use of Regular Expressions (RegEx) is quite common among software engineers and DevOps or IT roles where they specify a string pattern to match a specific string in a text. This can be used to perform wild-card fuzzy search to match and test occurrences of strings.

Often, programmers will use RegEx to validate that an input received from a user conforms to an expected condition. To list several examples:

1. Testing that a user's provided e-mail address is valid:

---

[39] https://github.com/mathiasbynens/cssesc
[40] https://github.com/mathiasbynens/CSS.escape
[41] https://www.npmjs.com/package/js-string-escape

```
1  var testEmail = /^([a-zA-Z0-9])(([\-.]|[_]+)?([a-zA-Z0-9]+))*(@){1}[a-z0-9]+[.]\
2  {1}(([a-z]{2,3})|([a-z]{2,3}[.]{1}[a-z]{2,3}))$/.exec('john@example.com');
```

1. Testing that a user's provided input is a valid ASCII alphanumeric text:

```
1  var testAlphanumeric = /^[a-zA-Z0-9]*$/.exec('abc123');
```

The risk that is inherent with the use of Regular Expressions is the computational resources that require to parse text and match a given pattern. A flawed Regular Expression pattern can be attacked in a manner where a provided user input for text to match will require an outstanding amount of CPU cycles to process the RegEx execution. Such an attack will render the application unresponsive, and thus is referred to as a ReDoS - Regular Expression Denial of Service.

A vulnerable Regular Expression is known as one which applies repetition to a repeating capturing group, and where the string to match is composed of a suffix of a valid matching pattern plus characters that aren't matching the capturing group. Reviewing this statement with an example makes things easier. Consider the following regular expression:

```
1  var badRegex = /^((abc)*)+$/;
```

The above regular expression attempts to find multiple occurrences of the string "abc", so that the following text snippets would match this regex:

- abc
- abcabc
- abcabcabc

The following text snippets which this regex attempts to match will fail:

- abca
- abc abc

To exploit this vulnerable regular expression an attacker can craft a matching text which is composed first of the suffix from a valid matching pattern, which means that "abc" is a valid pattern so it will begin with that. Following it, a char that begins the new pattern but isn't necessarily matching it - "a". Thus, a maliciously crafted regular expression is "abca". Almost. That's the idea, but that string is very small and the regular expression expansion that happens for every possibility is very small so this regular expression execution will finish very quickly.

Getting the CPU to work hard requires a longer string with more occurrences of the base capturing group "abc". An illustrative example is:

```
1  abc abc abc a
```

Thus "abc" is repeating and then ending with the char "a" which begins a new capturing group. However that example string is very small too and any modern CPU will quickly process through that as well. How about if a longer matching text is being evaluated?

Try the following:

```
1  var re = /^((abc)*)+$/;
2  console.log(re.exec('abcabcabcabcabcabcabcabcabcabcabcabcabcabcabcab\
3  cabcabcabcabcabcabcabcabcabca'));
```

Hopefully this did not run on a production server otherwise Node.js would've taken it's time to work through that. On my local development machine it actually took approximately 40 seconds as can be seen:

```
1  $ time node re.js
2  null
3  node re.js  41.88s user 0.00s system 99% cpu 41.883 total
```

There are many variations to a vulnerable regular expression, some examples taken from OWASP[42], and Wikipedia's ReDoS[43] pages are:

- (a|aa)+
- ([a-zA-Z]+)*

Hint

Try exploiting the above two examples by matching them on a text of many a's with an ending ! char. Also, the first example of an e-mail matching regular expression looks suspecious too.

---

[42] https://www.owasp.org/index.php/Regular_expression_Denial_of_Service_-_ReDoS
[43] https://en.wikipedia.org/wiki/ReDoS

Safe Regular Expressions

There is no magic to apply on regular expressions to make them safe, but rather the secret lies in crafting a correct, performant and safe regular expression pattern. Software engineers should pay attention for increased security implications when creating regular expressions.

Taking the above example of /^((abc)*)+$/ is simply a human error in writing a pattern, even though it works it's not safe to use. The same regular expression match would also work if the following pattern was used /^(abc)*$/, which is safe as it is not repeating a more complex sub-expression.

OWASP Validated RegEx

OWASP's website provides a short list of common validated regular expressions[44] which are safe to use as well as links to other useful RegEx resources.

Validator.js

validator.js[45] is the go-to library for validating user input. It is mature, well tested, and constantly being attacked with multiple attack vectors with an attempt to find flaws and fix them.

validator.js is suitable for both frontend JavaScript as well as Node.js server-side backend. Except from validating input, it also provides sanitization functions for specific input types and expected output.

Installing validator.js for Node.js:

```
npm install validator
```

Complete documentation for all available validation and sanitization functions is available in the project's README page on GitHub: https://github.com/chriso/validator.js[46].

validator.js only accepts strings as input and will otherwise throw an error. An example of validating that a user input is an expected e-mail address:

---

[44] https://www.owasp.org/index.php/OWASP_Validation_Regex_Repository
[45] https://github.com/chriso/validator.js
[46] https://github.com/chriso/validator.js

```
1  var validator = require('validator');
2  console.log(validator.isEmail('liran.tal@gmail.com'));
```

Safe-RegEx

safe-regex[47] is a library that can be used for both Node.js as well as frontend browsers to test whether a given regular expression pattern is potentially dangerous. The library hasn't been updated in a while, though it does check the very simple rule of repetitions of sub-expressions which is the primary rule for avoiding vulnerable regular expressions.

It is interesting to test the aforementioned e-mail validation regex that was mentioned in an example.

To begin with installing the library locally:

```
1  npm install safe-regex
```

And then testing a regex pattern:

```
1  var saferegex = require('safe-regex');
2  var emailRegex = /^([a-zA-Z0-9])(([\-.]|[_]+)?([a-zA-Z0-9]+))*(@){1}[a-z0-9]+[.]\
3  {1}(([a-z]{2,3})|([a-z]{2,3}[.]{1}[a-z]{2,3}))$/;
4
5  console.log(saferegex(emailRegex));
```

The console output would yield `false` as indeed this example of an e-mail validation rule is vulnerable to ReDoS attacks.

RegEx DoS

RegEx-Dos[48] is a command line tool that aids in searching for vulnerable regular expressions by scanning JavaScript files contents and testing any regular expression patterns with the [safe-regex] library.

It is a handy tool to add to any project on the DevOps pipeline or the build chain to confirm that no vulnerabilities are introduced, and if they do the fix is quick as they are found during the build stage.

---

[47] https://github.com/substack/safe-regex
[48] https://github.com/jagracey/RegEx-DoS

Strict Mode and Eval

Strict mode was introduced in ECMAScript 5.1[49] to enable a restricted version of JavaScript for enhanced security, and error management. It disables some language features which if used, may lead to confusion, inconsistency or security problems.

Some of them are:

- `eval` and `with` are disabled from being referred to as identifiers of any sort.
- Variables must be explicitly declared
- Property names can't be duplicated in an object definition, or in parameters passed to functions.
- Unwanted behavior will now throw errors

For ECMAScript 6, enabling strict mode has some more effect on the language syntax:

- No values can be set on primitive variables like Boolean, String, or Numbers.
- Octal values can be assigned to variables only using a "0o" syntax.

It is probable that you have witnessed the strict mode invocation as it became quite the de-facto for writing securely in JavaScript. It is recognized by programs that start with the following line:

```
'use strict';
```

It affects the entire script, or it can affect only a portion of it, such as a specific function if applied inside.

Eval

The `eval()` function is perhaps of the most frowned upon JavaScript pieces from a security perspective. It parses a JavaScript string as text, and executes it as if it were a JavaScript code. Mixing that with untrusted user input that might find it's way to `eval()` is a recipe for disaster that can end up with server compromise.

 The use of `eval()` isn't specific to JavaScript, but is also found in other programming languages such as PHP, Perl, and others.

While there is no inherent security flaw regarding the use of `eval()` in your code, it is often perceived as bad practice to make use of it. Cases where you might need to use eval are when it is required to

---
[49] http://www.ecma-international.org/ecma-262/5.1/#sec-10.1.1

dynamically run JavaScript code, such that is somehow generated, put together, and not owned by yourself. Otherwise, there's always the option to refactor the code and avoid using eval altogether.

 Who said it's evil?

The phrase "eval() is evil" is credited to Douglas Crockford[50], an active member in the evolution of the JavaScript language, and evangelist of the JSON standard.

Surprisingly enough, eval has friends: `setTimeout()` and `setInterval()` are also regarded as bad coding practices for the same reason that they both accept string as input, which they parse and evaluate for execution.

Cryptographic Practices

The use of cryptography functions is quite common when building web applications, and is often presenting the use case of maintaining a database of users and their passwords. Encrypting a user's password is another layer of defense to protect against server breach or data leakage through SQL Injection or other attacks.

Hash functions are commonly used for one-way cryptography, such that is used to protect a user's password.

Risk

There are many cryptographic hashing functions and algorithms which are available to use, but choosing the correct one is important as a best practice to make sure that encrypted data stays confidential even if it ended up as public content.

MD5[51] and SHA[52] are examples of commonly known cryptographic functions which are popular amongst developers to employ, yet they are quite insecure for encrypting data that is meant to remain confidential. The reasons behind this statement are:

1. These cryptographic hash functions are unsalted, which means they do not take into consideration per hash value randomness and uniqueness, therefore they are vulnerable to brute force attacks using pre-built dictionaries.
2. MD5 and SHA family of hash functions are very fast in computing a hash, which may seems as a performance feature, but on the other hand they also make it very easy and accessible for an attacker to enumerate such hash quite quickly.

---

[50] https://en.wikipedia.org/wiki/Douglas_Crockford
[51] http://en.wikipedia.org/wiki/MD5
[52] http://en.wikipedia.org/wiki/Secure_Hash_Algorithm

Rainbow Tables

rainbow tables[53] are pre-computed hash dictionaries for a variety of password policies, for example an alphanumeric 8 limit chars.

Writing up your own hash function is a bad practice, simply because there is so much science into a properly working secure hash and an individual can easily get it wrong. Further read on this topic is available on OWASP's Cryptographic Storage Cheat Sheet[54].

The Solution of Secure Hash Functions

To meet security standards we combine a proper hash function with an adequate algorithm which results in a secure hash function. What makes such a hash secure is that it employs the use of salts and are inherently slower so that brute force attacks or dictionary lookups are not worth the effort. Other characteristics makes them secure such as iterating the hash millions of times.

bcrypt[55] is a commonly accepted secure hash function which employs the Blowfish cipher. When using bcrypt with Node.js, one should consider the use of native bcrypt libraries which offer superior performance verses the JavaScript implementation which are slower, yet are cross-platform compatible.

JavaScript bcrypt implementations

Other options to consider for a JavaScript implementation are bcrypt.js[56].

Using Node.js native bcrypt we will first install it via npm:

```
npm install bcrypt
```

The choice for bcrypt[57] library is due to it's native C++ bindings which makes this library very performant and thus recommended to use on production servers. It is straightforward to install it on a GNU/Linux OS, however Windows or Mac users will need to meet some dependencies requirements[58]. To make it easy for Windows or Mac users, you can use the aforementioned bcrypt.js[59] library which is a plain JavaScript implementation and compatible with the native bcrypt library.

bcrypt provides the following primary methods which work asynchronously:

---

[53] http://en.wikipedia.org/wiki/Rainbow_table
[54] https://www.owasp.org/index.php/Cryptographic_Storage_Cheat_Sheet
[55] https://en.wikipedia.org/wiki/Bcrypt
[56] https://github.com/dcodeIO/bcrypt.js/
[57] https://en.wikipedia.org/wiki/Bcrypt
[58] https://github.com/kelektiv/node.bcrypt.js#dependencies
[59] https://github.com/dcodeIO/bcrypt.js/

- `bcrypt.genSalt(saltRounds, callback(err, salt))` - `genSalt` generates a salt, and can iterate `saltRounds` number of times to further increase salt randomness, taking a `callback` function with an error object as the first argument, or the generated salt in the 2nd argument.
- `bcrypt.hash(password, salt, callback(err, hash))` - `hash` generates a hash from the an input `password` argument using a `salt`. If `salt` is a number, it uses it as a rounds count to create a salt on it's own. Once a hash is generated, it calls a `callback` function with an error object as the first argument, or the generated hash in the 2nd argument.
- `bcrypt.compare(password, hashedPassword, callback(err, res))` - `compare` will compare a given password with a given hash and will call a callback function with an error object as the first argument, or a boolean `res` object if there's a match.

When hashing passwords, it is important to understand the cost of the salt rounds count. The following table provides a reference based on my quad core i5-3470 CPU @ 3.20GHz:

salt rounds	password generation time
2	2ms
8	17ms
10	68ms
11	132ms
12	263ms
13	526ms
14	1s
15	2s
17	8s
19	33s
20	1m

When choosing a salt round count one must take into account that CPU power increases in a very fast pace (see Moore's law[60]), and at the end of the day CPU power can be bought so it ends up to be a matter of how much money to invest in attempting to crack a password (imagine a person buying a cluster of CPUs from a cloud service like Amazon or Google just to crack a password).

For this reason, the number of rounds count will change as hardware will become more powerful. A general guideline would be to set a round count to anything between 0.2 seconds to 1 second for a non mission critical web application, depending on your personal paranoia level (PPL).

Creating a hash for a password with bcrypt:

---

[60] https://en.wikipedia.org/wiki/Moore%27s_law

```
1  var bcrypt = require('bcrypt');
2
3  bcrypt.hash("hacktheplanet", 13, function(err, hash) {
4    console.log(hash);
5  });
```

To authenticate the user, it is required to simply compare the original password with it's previously computed hash:

```
1  var bcrypt = require('bcrypt');
2
3  bcrypt.compare("hacktheplanet", hash, function(err, res) {
4    if (!!res) {
5      console.log('password match!');
6    } else {
7      console.log('wrong password');
8    }
9  });
```

bcrypt features a synchronous set of functions for the same aforementioned methods: `genSaltSync`, `hashSync`, and `compareSync`. some input/output limitations with bcrypt are truncating after 72 chars, and allows an input password of up to 51 chars.

While a synchronous set of implementation might seem appealing due to the simple nature of code flow, an adept Node.js developer will take into account the fact for Node.js being a single-threaded platform. This comes in to play when a developer might invoke a 10 rounds `hashSync` function call which "eats" about 50ms of CPU time and that means that the event loop is stalling **all** requests to the Node.js server for 50ms.

 Available Secure Hash Functions

There are other secure hash functions than bcrypt: Argon2 which is the *new kid on the block*, scrypt, and last as well as least preferred PBKDF2.

User Process Privileges

Running web servers which serve requests from an untrusted and open public medium brings with it an inherent risk where malicious attempts will try to compromise the underlying server and operating system through vulnerabilities in the web server.

Web servers have no reason to operate with a super-user privilege level, except for being able to bind and listen for incoming requests on port 80 or 443 which are allowed only to the super-user in

Linux and UNIX variants (non super-users may bind to ports larger than 1024 on those operation systems).

To mitigate this issue, production environments often feature a more secured medium to handle requests and proxy them to the web server that binds on another port using a regular system user.

Such medium may vary in purpose and can be identified usually as one of the following, but not limited to:

1. A Reverse Proxy
2. A Load Balancer

Using a Load Balancer for example, it will most probably terminate the SSL connection to offload this heavy CPU work from web servers, and expose a routable IP and host to the public to access it over a secure HTTP channel. All incoming requests are routed to Node.js web application servers that are not directly exposed outside.

These Node.js servers would ideally run without a super-user owner, which is why many Node.js frameworks and server setup guides will feature a server that listens on high ports such as 3000, 4000, 5000, 8888, and 9000. This is so that the server can be executed without requiring a super-user privilege. If the Node.js server is exploited then it doesn't compromise the entire server just from it's own share of OS resources, unless a privilege escalation vulnerability exists.

Summary

Keeping a security-oriented state of mind while writing code and setting up environments is an essential layer of security. Secure code guidelines may vary in different organizations depending on culture, technology stack and other considerations but they should be followed nonetheless.

While not presuming to be a complete list, in this chapter we reviewed the following topics for security best practices and guidelines:

- Input validation
- Output encoding
- Regular Expressions
- JavaScript's Strict Mode
- Cryptographic Practices
- User Process Privileges

Injection Flaws

Injection attacks exploit vulnerabilities in systems and applications that fail to validate, escape, and secure their methods of utilizing other sub-systems. Such injection flaws apply to many components, among the most popular are SQL injections, and Operating System injection.

Increased security awareness when developing software is essential to mitigate such attacks. Following best practices and secure code helps mitigate injection vulnerabilities as follows:

- **Validation** - confirm that when passing data to a sub-system it confirms to an expected type or format
- **Escaping or Encoding** - always escape or encode data when passing to a sub-system to ensure it is handled properly

Making use of these practices in each component differs. Taking SQL Injections as an example, an implementation of the Escaping or Encoding rule is implied by the use of Prepared Statements or also known as Parameters Binding technique, which ensures that the at an SQL level, the data is properly escaped and appended to an SQL query.

Elaborate read
More information about this topic can be found on OWASP's injections flaws[61] section.

NoSQL Injections

Similar to SQL injections, improper validation or escaping of user manipulated input can lead to dynamic queries that are executed on NoSQL databases.

Due to the different nature of SQL and NoSQL databases, the attack vector isn't necessarily the same. For example, a common user input such as illustrated below will not have an affect on a NoSQL database even if the malicious user input has not been properly sanitized or escaped:

NoSQL query to validate user login credentials:

```
db.users.findOne({username: username, password: password});
```

Assuming an attacker knows that a valid username exists as "admin", a malicious user input for the username field would be:

---

[61] https://www.owasp.org/index.php/Injection_Flaws

```
1   admin' --
```

The above examples illustrates an attempt to alter the original query the programmer wrote, although this will not have any catastrophic affects on a NoSQL database such as MongoDB. This is because the basic structure of the query language is entirely different.

On the other hand, if this input was to run on an SQL database which doesn't properly validate or escape strings, then the result would be as follows:

```
1   -- Original query in code:
2   -- SELECT id, user FROM users WHERE username = '$username' AND password = '$pass\
3   word'
4   --
5   -- The altered query based on the user input:
6   SELECT id, user FROM users WHERE username = 'admin' -- AND password = ''
```

The Risk

ExpressJS by default will not provide a mechanism to access any data sent in a non-GET request, which is an obvious problem when implementing simple things such as login forms which send form data or a JSON POST request. To quote the official guide[62] on expressjs.com on this:

> req.body contains key-value pairs of data submitted in the request body. By default, it is undefined, and is populated when you use body-parsing middleware such as body-parser and multer.

This is where the `body-parser` library comes in. It makes it available to parse non-GET query data and it is widely used today in the majority of ExpressJS projects as the standard way of accessing requests body payload. In-fact it is so popular that as of writing this book, the body-parser library has been downloaded for roughly 5 million times just this past month.

body-parser has two main parsing middlewares which are described as follows:

- `bodyParser.json()` - this middleware is designed to parse JSON payload that is sent over an `application/json` content type.
- `bodyParser.urlencoded()` - this middleware is designed to parse form field payloads which are common to HTML page implementations that get sent over an `application/x-www-form-urlencoded` content type.

With either of these parsing methods enabled, the result is that body-parser populates the `req.body` object with property names, based on the payload that got sent on the request.

In the case of the `.json()` method it will further attempt to convert any strings to actual objects that will populate `req.body`.

---
[62] http://expressjs.com/en/api.html

Re-constructing a NoSQL Injection

A typical application will expect to receive the username and password fields either as a normal HTML FORM submit or through an AJAX call where the request sends these fields as a JSON content-type.

In this case, an ExpressJS web application will require the following middlewares:

```
app.use(bodyParser.json());
app.use(bodyParser.urlencoded());
```

To authenticate the user, a typical POST login route and matching the request sent from the browser to the database would look similar to the following:

```
app.post('/login', function(req, res) {
  User.find({ username: req.body.username, password: req.body.password }, functi\
on(err, users) {
    res.status(200).send(users);
  });
});
```

In the above code, the `User` model runs a query to to the MongoDB database to match the username and pasword fields. They are populated in the `req.body` object as first citizens JavaScript properties.

If a malicious user would take advantage of this type of authentication matching logic then they can exploit MongoDB's operators to return a valid `users` object. This can be accomplished by sending the following JSON data as the login POST request:

```
{"username":{"$gt": ""}, "password":{"$gt": ""}}
```

This works because `req.body.username` will be set to the object `{"$gt": ""}` which is a valid MongoDB operator to match any documents where the `username` field is not empty (the `$gt` operator means "greater than").

This can be validated easily with the following curl request:

```
curl -X POST -H "Content-Type: application/json" --data '{"username":{"$gt": ""}\
, "password":{"$gt": ""}}' http://localhost:31337/login
```

Threats

Beyond the obvious noSQL injection that can lead to bypassing user authentication, there are severe threats to a MongoDB server such as Denial of Service (DOS) attacks where an attacker would deliberately inject a complicated RegEx or matching statement that will throw MongoDB into CPU resource hogging actions such as full table scans.

Another security threat is related to privacy and data leakage where an attacker can provide a RegEx value that will match many records in order to pull out information from the MongoDB server.

The Solution

To prevent NoSQL injections it is required to validate the user input or escape it properly. Additionally, some Node.js libraries like sequelize[63] ORM provide prepared statements for queries.

A very first and basic step is to validate user input, with regards to the following rules to confirm the expected type being received in the request is valid:

1. Validate length and type of the data
2. Validate and sanitize the input to an expected type (for example, type casting)

To mitigate the above NoSQL injection vulnerability a simple fix to our code is needed - casting the username and password fields to a string.

The fix is illustrated in the following code snippet:

```
app.post('/login', function(req, res) {

  // coerce the req.body properties into strings, resulting in [object object] i\
n case
  // of a converted object instead of a real string
  // another convention is to call the object's .toString();
  User.find({ username: String(req.body.username), password: String(req.body.pas\
sword) }, function(err, users) {
      res.status(200).send(users);
  });
});
```

If our application expects usernames and passwords to be only strings, then nothing breaks. Yet, let's investigate what happens when we cast the object {"$gt": ""} to a string:

```
console.log(String({"$gt": ""}));
// result is: '[object Object]'
```

In conclusion, there are many ways to validate and confirm the expected input type is being matched so keeping track of how MongoDB queries are run with regards to the input they match against is crucial. One example is the passport-local[64] library which completely ignores the request if the data it received is an object.

---

[63] http://sequelizejs.com
[64] https://github.com/jaredhanson/passport-local

NoSQL SSJS Injections

Server-side JavaScript (SSJS) Injection occurs when a server-side component allows the execution of arbitrary JavaScript code in the server context. It may allow this to provide some extended functionality, but nevertheless, this capability opens the door for untrusted input data by the user to be interpreted and executed.

Common server-side JavaScript injections can be referred to any use of eval(), setTimeout(), setInterval(), or, Function(). All of which, allow parsing arguments which may wrongly originate from a user controlled input data.

MongoDB's Evaluation Query operator, referred to as $where allows to match documents when they satisfy a JavaScript expression.

Let's review an example of such query for a MongoDB database:

```
> db.users.find( { $where: function() { return (this.country == 'IL'); }});
```

When executed, MongoDB matches all the user's collection documents where their country field equals to the string 'IL' and will return all those matches. This can also be shortened and written as follows:

```
> db.users.find( { $where: this.country == 'IL' }});
```

The Risk

A security vulnerability can be introduced when un-sanitized parameters are passed to the evaluated JavaScript expression for the $where operator.

The following is a very stripped down version of this vulnerability when exploited by an attacker. It demonstrates an ExpressJS application that defined a /userCountries GET API which executes a MongoDB injection with a $where operator:

```
app.get('/userCountries', function(req, res) {

  var country = req.query.country;
  var searchCriteria = "this.country == " + "'" + country + "'";

  users.find({
    $where: searchCriteria
  }).toArray(function(err, response) {

    res.render('users', { users: response });
```

```
11
12    });
13  });
```

The `searchCriteria` variable will build the where expression based on user input, and so the exact MongoDB query that will execute will look as follows:

```
1    $where: "this.country == 'IL'"
```

This query awfully resembles traditional SQL injections, and because the $where operator evaluates JavaScript then such insecure method of combining user input with a MongoDB query may result in the following malicious scenario:

An attacker sends a GET request which satisfies the $where operator by providing text to the boolean expression and also closing it with a single quote. Now, it is possible to terminate this string expression and add any valid JavaScript code. Finally, there's a closing single quote that gets concatenated to the string, so the GET request also adds it.

```
1    $ curl "http://localhost:31337/user?country=IL';while(true)\{\};'"
```

The resulting $where operator expression looks as follows:

```
1    $where: "this.country == 'IL';while(true){};''"
```

This valid JavaScript expression is actually triggering a DoS attack on the MongoDB service. While Node.js isn't exploited here and can further serve requests, any additional requests to the Node.js server that require MongoDB will stall. At this point, MongoDB is completely taking up 100% CPU resources in an infinite loop that will end only when watchdogs and timers kick-in.

The Solution

In reference to MongoDB itself, the `$where` operator should probably be avoided when possible. The documentation[65] further elaborates the insecure and inefficient characteristics of the $where operator. It should only be used as a last resort.

Follow these general guidelines to avoid and mitigate NoSQL injection attacks: * Sanitizing and validating user input - do not allow user originating input as is. Always validate, and filter to match the allowed and expected data. * Prepared statements - familiar from traditional SQL methodologies, secure the data passed to queries through prepared statements. Better alternative to the official MongoDB client are ORM and ODMs that provide out of the box security. For example, sequelizejs[66], or mongoose[67]. * Don't use insecure JavaScript functions to parse user input, such as: `eval()`, `setTimeout()`, `setInterval()`, and `Function()`.

---

[65] https://docs.mongodb.com/manual/reference/operator/query/where/
[66] https://github.com/sequelize/sequelize
[67] https://github.com/Automattic/mongoose

Blind NoSQL Injections

The concept behind the blind injection attack is to extract as much information as possible from the database so that even if a direct noSQL injection fails, the database exposes correct and incorrect noSQL statements differently to the user, thus allowing to collect information by sending varying requests.

A close variant to blind noSQL injection exists in MongoDB through the use of it's operators. One of which is the $regex operator which allows to gather information based on varying regular expressions sent as input data to the database.

The Risk

In the previous section about noSQL Injections we visited a naive example where both the username and password inputs are tested on the database, such as:

```
User.find({ username: req.body.username, password: req.body.password}, function(\
err, document) {})
```

With the risks and solutions for the above query made clear, one might assume that the next evolutionary step in constructing the user and password validation logic would be to validate the password input vs the actual password stored in the database.

One approach would be to just find the user record and once found, invoke a callback function to validate the passwords match. An example of doing this is as follows:

```
function userAuth(req) {
    Users.findOne({username: req.body.username}, compareUserPass);

    function compareUserPass(err, dbUserRecord) {
        return dbUserRecord.password === req.body.password;

        // Tip: next time compare a provided password to a stored hash
        // in the database, so that you never store plaintext passwords.
    }
}
```

The supposedly enhanced security is achieved by comparing a plaintext password in the database with the plaintext input from the user. Implementing the above would mitigate an input such as {username: {"$gt": ""}, password: {"$gt": ""}} because even if a user is hit from the database due to the $gt operator, the passwords are actually compared and expected to be the same.

The Attack

What seems like a working solution should still raise a red flag, especially the username being used without being sanitized first.

Because the password is compared to find an identical match, an attack vector would be to blindly try to match a record with a specific password. If the username is indeed un-santizied we can employ other MongoDB operators to find user records based on specific patterns by ending the following query:

```
curl -X POST -H "Content-Type: application/json" --data '{"username":{"regex": "\
demo"}, "password":"123456"}' http://localhost:31337/login
```

If an account exists which username is demo and password is 123456 (which is the most used password in 2017[68]), then a new valid session will be created and we successfully exploited the database.

In real systems, there would probably be many user accounts registered on the system, hence a simple "demo" regex might not be suffice. Imagine the following usernames:

1. test_demo
2. user_demo
3. demo1
4. demo2

And so on... the Blind NoSQL Injection is thus employed by blindly sending varying requests to try and match an account record so the input payload differs on each request, such as:

- {"username": {"regex": "^demo$"}, "password": "123456"}
- {"username": {"regex": "^demo1$"}, "password": "123456"}
- {"username": {"regex": "^demo2$"}, "password": "123456"}

The Solution

Understanding of why Blind NoSQL Injection works is necessary to mitigate such attacks.

At the very least, all input must be validated and sanitized before sent to the database, as we reviewed in earlier sections.

---

[68] http://www.telegraph.co.uk/technology/2017/01/16/worlds-common-passwords-revealed-using

OS Command Injection

Care consideration must be given when resorting to the undesired option of executing Operating System (OS) commands to execute a program, or shell script. While there may be valid reasons for doing so in some situations, the potential for a critical security vulnerability is great because of the OS-level context. When this is done incorrectly, it may lead to OS command injection and thus compromising the underlying server OS.

In similar to other injection vulnerabilities, the focus on mitigating this kind of attack is to use a proper string binding with a secure shell execution function call, and apply proper output encoding, which in this case is in the context of an Operating System command shell.

Node.js provides OS command execution using child processes set of functions, and specifically using the `child_process` module. The `child_process.exec()` function allows to spawn a shell and then execute a given command within that shell context. Taking into account the following example:

```
var child_process = require('child_process');

function listPath(directory) {
  var cmd = "ls -alh";
  child_process.exec(cmd + ' ' + directory, function(err, data) {
    console.log(data);
  });
}
```

In the above code snippet, the `listPath` function takes a directory reference as a parameter and appends it to the command that gets executed in a shell. The `directory` parameter to the function should be regarded as an untrusted source, such as one that originates from untrusted user input. What would happen if that parameter will be set to ; `cat /etc/passwd` ? Similar to how SQL injection attacks work, the special semi-colon char will end one command statement, and begin a new one, leading to an execution as follows:

```
$ ls -alh
$ cat /etc/passwd
```

Due to this vulnerability, the `child_process.exec()` function should be avoided entirely at all circumstances, and instead one should make use of `child_process.execFile()`, which executes a single and bound command, and allows passing it any number of arguments that cannot be altered and spawned as individual commands.

Thus, a safe command execution methodology:

```
1  var child_process = require('child_process');
2
3  function listPath(directory) {
4    var cmd = "ls";
5    var cmdParams = ['ls'];
6    cmdParams.push(directory);
7    child_process.execFile(cmd, cmdParams, function(err, data) {
8      console.log(data);
9    });
10 }
```

By no means, should the execFile() function leave a comfort feeling of safety. Some Linux OS shell commands do allow invoking other programs from their own execution, so just limiting the passing of parameters to that command is not helpful.

 Avoid when possible

Avoid at all costs executing arbitrary commands from within your Node.js program. In the last resort when that is required, always make use of execFile function call, and only to known and well-understood OS commands which can not be tricked into running commands passed in parameters.

Summary

Injection attacks aren't always easy to defect against, which makes them one of the top ranking OWASP vulnerabilities. They require understanding of the context the code is executed in, ability to escape the data correctly, and implementing it correctly and getting it right isn't straightforward.

The bread and butter of safely mitigating injection attacks are properly validating user input, and properly escaping it. Master these through out all layers of your application to follow the security in depth paradigm.

OWASP Injection reading

OWASP features good resources to learn and extend your knowledge further on injection attacks, amongst them are the basic injection theory[69] guide, and the injection prevention cheat sheet[70]

---

[69] https://www.owasp.org/index.php/Injection_Theory
[70] https://www.owasp.org/index.php/Injection_Prevention_Cheat_Sheet

Secure Dependency Management

Node.js, being modular in nature, inherently makes projects heavily dependent on external libraries. Having external dependencies in your project is not a bad thing per say, but it requires a great deal of attention and awareness as you may be subject to vulnerabilities that are introduced by those external libraries.

On dependencies

Some projects are small that they truly require no dependency, others may require just a few, yet is is almost impossible in these days of the "JavaScript Fatigue" state to not rely on external dependencies, even those that are required to build and develop the project.

3rd Party dependencies are not unique to Node.js. In fact, other platforms and languages like Java, Ruby, PHP and Python promote a modular architecture and heavily rely on community or commercial libraries to build projects.

Node.js packages are hosted and managed by a project called npm[71], which became the biggest package repository already in 2014. The current state of packages count is illustrated thanks to modulecounts[72] where it is compared with other platform and languages, true to end of 2016 year:

---

[71] https://www.npmjs.com/
[72] http://www.modulecounts.com/

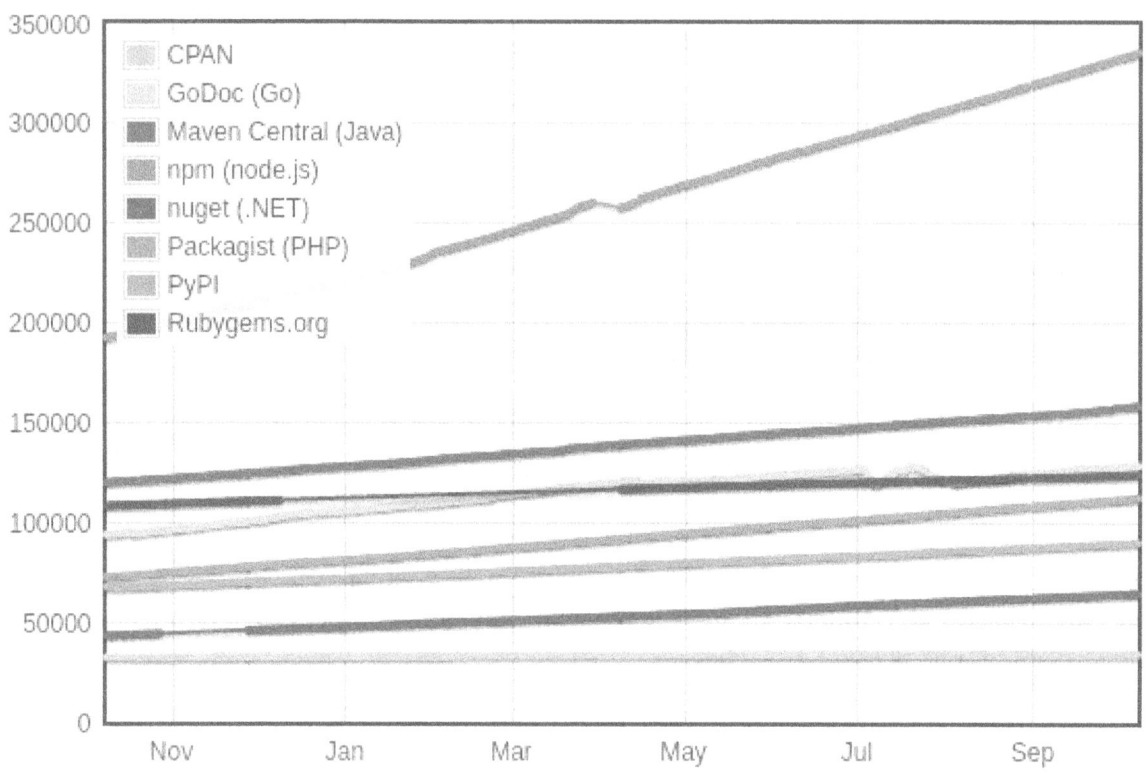

npm pacakge repository comparison

 npm stands for...

Actually, npm is not an abbreviation for 'node package manager' as some people tend to presume. It isn't an abbreviation for anything, it's just npm.

Evaluating Dependencies

Understanding your dependency tree, and your dependencies dependencies is a vital action that needs careful review to ensure that the libraries you intend to use are mature, and of high quality.

When we reviewed the libraries in this book we presented the project's badges to present the maturity and quality level of the project. With the plethora of Node.js packages, it's easy to mistaken pick an outdated, unmaintained or otherwise low quality project.

Taking ExpressJS[73] project as an example, let's review the npm pacakge page for it which reveals useful information and can help to evaluate a package https://www.npmjs.com/package/express.

---

[73] https://www.npmjs.com/package/express

Project Activity

A general project activity shows information about the maintainers and collaborators, it's last releases and a quick link to the GitHub project page:

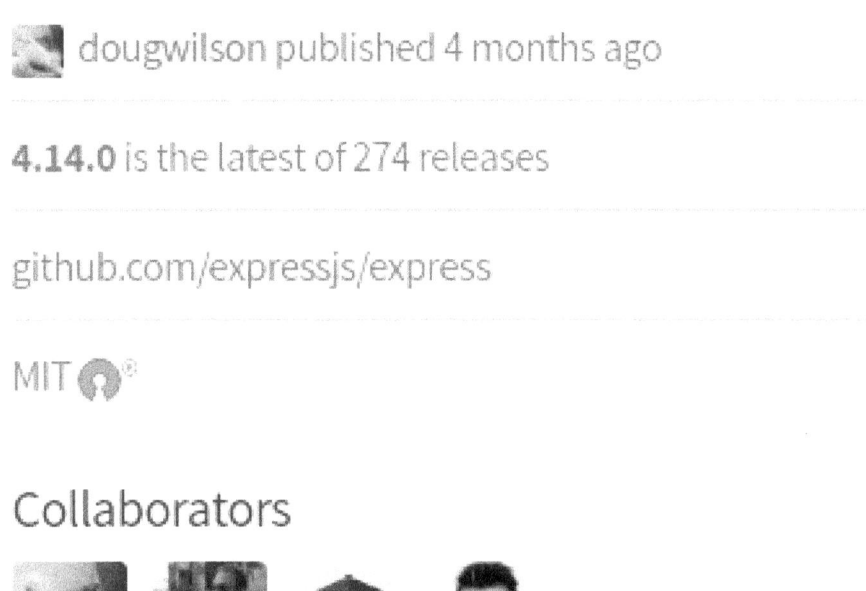

expressjs npm project activity

Project Statistics

Curious about the project's popularity can be settled by reviewing the download statistics for ExpressJS, which also features numbers it pulls from GitHub with regards to open issues, and open pull requests:

Stats

250,490 downloads in the last day

1,660,740 downloads in the last week

7,372,294 downloads in the last month

88 open issues on GitHub

37 open pull requests on GitHub

expressjs npm project statistics

Project Dependencies

The project's own dependencies are listed, as well as other npm packages which depend upon the ExpressJS library itself (which is a bigger count than possible to git in the picture below):

Dependencies (26)

vary, utils-merge, type-is, serve-static, send, range-parser, qs, proxy-addr, path-to-regexp, parseurl, on-finished, methods, merge-descriptors, fresh, finalhandler, etag, escape-html, encodeurl, depd, debug, cookie-signature, cookie, content-type, content-disposition, array-flatten, accepts

Dependents

experience, musivk, lmd, entangled, rpc-duplex-node, powerstone, web-tracer, express-toybox, bare-auth, @tlrg/cookie-handshake, scio, psjs, frodo-downloader, fh-dev-proxy, qlik-auth-file, static-proxy, vue-dashing-js, ks_remote, webvr360, j2csv, radellite, express-waf, myexpress, isomagic, www-entu, saucier-core, slack-memebot, cf-launcher, testing-jfrog5, stratium-search-test, telegram-bot-express,

expressjs npm project dependencies

Dependency Tracking

External dependencies add the overhead of tracking the security of 3rd party libraries that are part of your project. We'll review several tools and techniques to keep track of the security status for your project dependencies.

A Project's Dependencies

For Node.js projects, dependencies split between your project's primary dependencies which are found in the dependencies property in the package.json file, as well as the dependencies required to build, develop and maintain the project, and are found in the devDependencies property. It is essential to track both and confirm none introduce a security vulnerability.

Node Security: nsp

nsp[74] is a command-line tool that helps track the security of project dependencies by detecting if they are subject to known vulnerabilities. It is one of the first Node.js tools in the information security ecosystem from the company [^lift security](https://liftsecurity.io/), which have been actively involved in Node.js and security in specific.

nsp builds it's database of vulnerabilities based on NIST National Vulnerability Database[75] as well as it's own repository of advisories[76]. It scans project dependencies based on the package.json file to compare versions of the installed libraries with known vulnerable versions based on the aforementioned databases.

It is customary to install nsp as a global module so it can be used in multiple projects:

```
npm install -g nsp
```

Running a security check for an existing Node.js project:

```
nsp check
```

A real output of a scan will look something like the following:

	Regular Expression Denial of Service
Name	minimatch
Installed	0.3.0
Vulnerable	<=3.0.1
Patched	>=3.0.2
Path	meanjs@0.5.0-beta > grunt-cli@0.1.13 > findup-sync@0.1.3 > glob@3.2.11 > minimatch@0.3.0
More Info	https://nodesecurity.io/advisories/118

nsp check scan

In the above report nsp detected a security issue in the meanjs project. The dependency grunt-cli introduces a vulnerable package called minimatch. It is required to upgrade to a newer version

---

[74]https://www.npmjs.com/package/nsp
[75]https://nvd.nist.gov/
[76]https://nodesecurity.io/advisories

of `grunt-cli` to receive an updated, patched version of `minimatch` as well (this is not guaranteed though).

 Report output

nsp supports different types of reporting output such as a summary, json output and others so it can be easily integrated with other automation and build tools if necessary.

nsp has grown beyond a command-line tool and is part of an ecosystem and cloud offering called Node Security Platform[77] that integrates with GitHub public or private repositories to track them and their pull-requests and ensure no insecure dependencies are being introduced to the project.

Snyk

Snyk[78] is a service for continuously monitoring your project's dependencies for any known vulnerabilities. Snyk provides a command-line interface, as well as a robust GitHub integration that can further simplify the process.

Snyk tests dependencies agains their open-source vulnerability database[79], and has dedicated researchers actively discovering new vulnerabilities to be disclosed. Similar to nsp (Node Security Platform), Snyk's GitHub integration scans a projects `package.json` to see what versions of dependencies are currently installed, and compares those versions to their database. The command-line interface goes a step further and scans the installed packages themselves.

To use the command-line interface, you first install Snyk as a global module:

```
npm install -g snyk
```

With the Snyk tool installed, you can test your project for vulnerabilities using the `snyk test` command:

```
snyk test
```

Snyk will test your installed packages against their vulnerability database and output something like the following:

---

[77] https://nodesecurity.io/
[78] https://snyk.io
[79] https://snyk.io/vuln/

```
x Low severity vulnerability found on hawk@1.1.1
- desc: Regular Expression Denial of Service
- info: https://snyk.io/vuln/npm:hawk:20160119
- from: goof@0.0.2 > tap@5.8.0 > codecov.io@0.1.6 > request@2.42.0 > hawk@1.1.1
No direct dependency upgrade can address this issue.
Run `snyk wizard` to explore remediation options.

x Medium severity vulnerability found on request@2.42.0
- desc: Remote Memory Exposure
- info: https://snyk.io/vuln/npm:request:20160119
- from: goof@0.0.2 > tap@5.8.0 > codecov.io@0.1.6 > request@2.42.0
No direct dependency upgrade can address this issue.
Run `snyk wizard` to explore remediation options.

Tested 519 dependencies for known vulnerabilities, found 2 vulnerabilities, 2 vulnerable paths.
```

snyk test scan

In this example, you can see that Snyk found two vulnerabilities. For each vulnerability, Snyk provides information about the serverity, a link to a detailed description, and the path through which the vulnerable package got into your system.

Snyk also prompts you to run `snyk wizard` which will walk you through the process of fixing those vulnerabilities. Before you do that, you'll want to authenticate using the authorization token you receive when you first sign up for the service. This ensures you won't run into any API rate limits, and also enables you to setup continuous monitoring, which we'll talk about shortly.

```
1  snyk auth <your token>
```

Now authorized, you can run the wizard to help you fix the issues Snyk found.

```
1  snyk wizard
```

The wizard will once again test your packages for vulnerabilities. For each vulnerability, you'll be prompted with all the same information you received when you ran `snyk test`. You'll also be provided with remediation options, like so:

```
Querying vulnerabilities database...
Tested 519 dependencies for known vulnerabilities, found 2 vulnerabilities, 2 vulnerable paths.

? Low severity vuln found in hawk@1.1.1, introduced via tap@5.8.0
- desc: Regular Expression Denial of Service
- info: https://snyk.io/vuln/npm:hawk:20160119
- from: tap@5.8.0 > codecov.io@0.1.6 > request@2.42.0 > hawk@1.1.1
  Remediation options (Use arrow keys)
  Upgrade (no sufficient upgrade available we'll notify you when there is one)
> Patch (modifies files locally, updates policy for `snyk protect` runs)
  Set to ignore for 30 days (updates policy)
  Skip
```

snyk wizard

In the above example, you can see that for Snyk is providing a few options for how to address the low severity vulnerability found in the hawk package, which in turn was introduced via the tap package. The basic options are to:

- Upgrade the package to a version where the vulnerability has been fixed. In this case, there is no upgrade that address the issue, which Snyk notes.
- Patch the issue, which modifies the actual files locally on your machine.
- Ignore the issue for 30 days, which will ensure that Snyk won't alert you to this vulnerability in subsequent tests until that 30 days has passed.
- Skip the issue altogether. If you choose to skip, Snyk will still report this issue each time it is run.

Once you've walked through the wizard for each discovered vulnerability, Snyk will apply any patches and upgrades you've selected (modifying package.json and running npm update as needed) and store your decisions in .snyk policy file that it will refer to whenever you run Snyk on that project in the future.

Since you've authenticated, a snapshot of the current state of your dependencies will also be stored to your account.

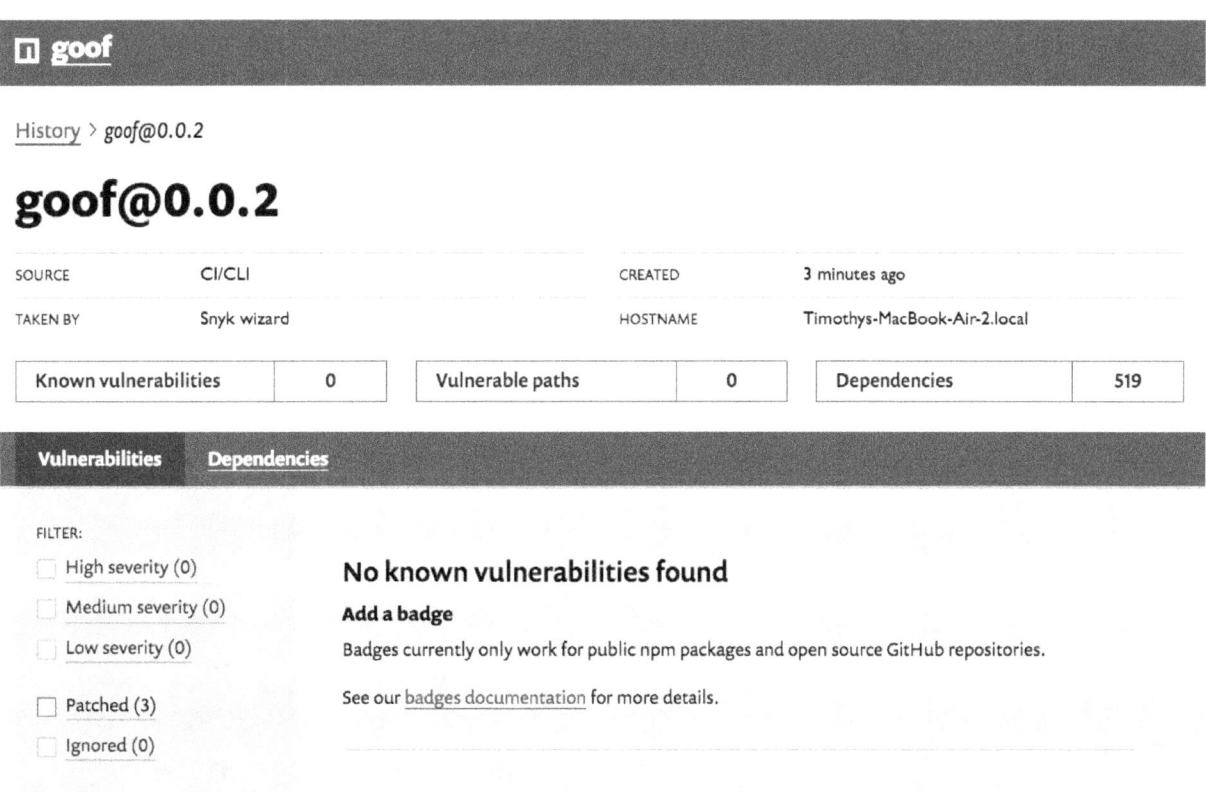

snapshot of your project on Snyk.io

This enables Snyk to notify you (using email or Slack) whenever a newly discovered vulnerability impacts your project, letting you address the issue immediately.

As part of the `wizard` process, Snyk will also optionally integrate some tests and protection steps into your `package.json` file. If you decide, you can:

- Have Snyk add `snyk test` to the `test` script, which will query local dependencies for vulnerabilities and throw an error if any are found.
- Have Snyk add `snyk protect` to your project as a `post-install` step. This way if you publish the module, Snyk can apply any patches you've selected each time the module is installed.

Snyk's command-line interface is great for integrating into your continuous integration systems, but an even more automated process is provided if your application is contained in a GitHub repository.

When you login to your Snyk account, there is a button allowing you to test your GitHub repositories. After you provide Snyk GitHub permissions, Snyk will automatically test these repos and provide the test results in an abbreviate form.

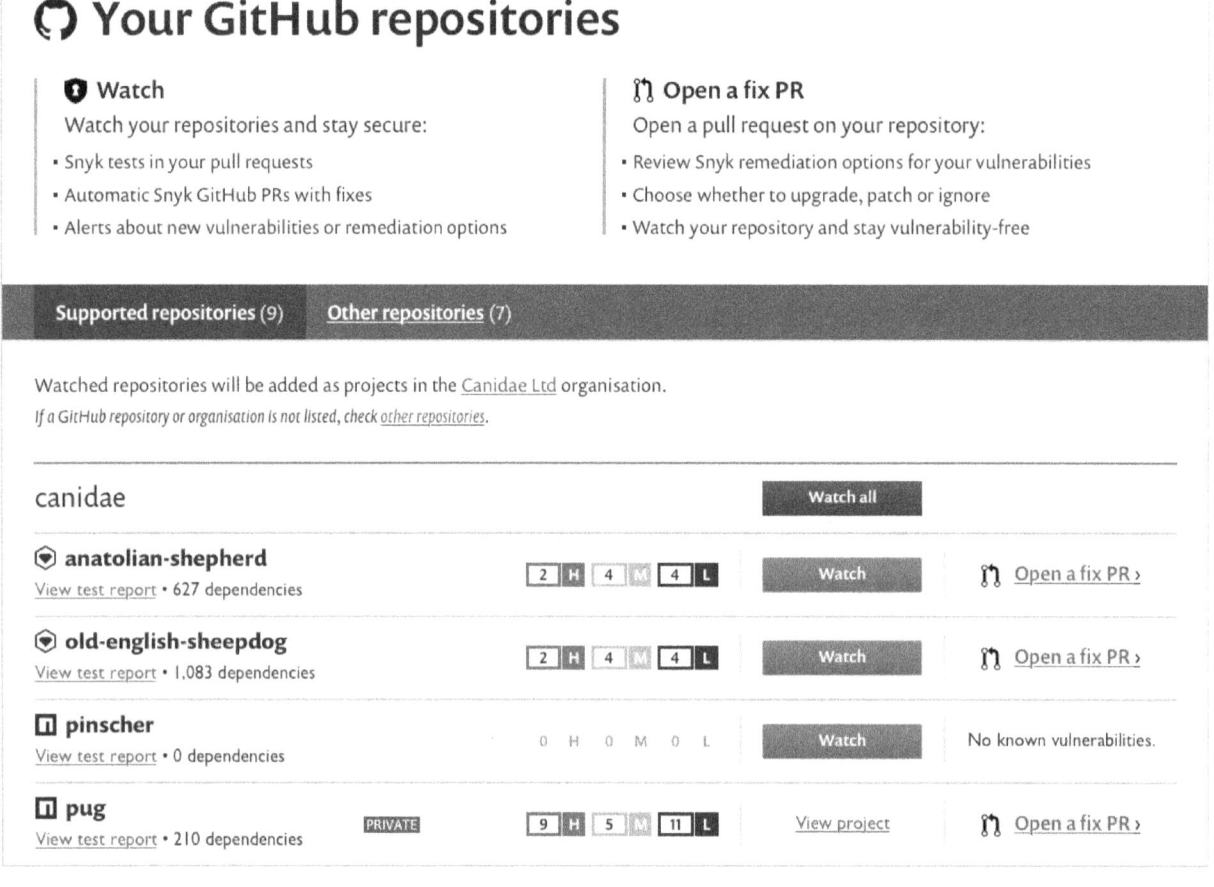

snyk GitHub integration

You can see in the screenshot above that for each repository, Snyk will tell you the number of high, medium and low priority vulnerabilities, as well as give you the option to "Watch" the repo. Selecting this will add the repository as a project to Snyk so that Snyk can continuously check it against any newly disclosed vulnerabilities.

You also have the option to "Open a fix PR". This will take you to a page where you can review the suggested remediations and create an automated pull request to your project with the required upgrades and patches.

snyk GitHub PR

The Snyk service is free for any open-source projects, with different tiers available for private projects depending on the functionality you need.

NPM Shrinkwrap

When publishing packages to npm, it is required to maintain semantic versioning[80] which is a program version specification[81] that defines how to properly version software releases.

In short, a version can and should be described by three identifiers: a major, a minor, and a patch. For example: 1.2.0. Keeping with the semver rules, a bug fix applied to a release should increment the patch version to 1.2.1. If a breaking API change occurred during a release then the major version should be incremented, thus resulting in a new version say 2.0.0.

When installing packages, npm automatically applies a range operator. This results in the package.json file having entries such as:

```
{
  "dependencies": {
    "library1": "~2.0.0",
    "library2": "^3.0.0"
  }
}
```

These tilde and caret operators define a version range for npm to look for new packages. If there is a new 2.0.1 release of *library1* then invoking an `npm install` will update the currently installed version to 2.0.1. For *library2* this is true as well, if a new 3.5.0 is released as well.

 Interactive Version Calculator

npm hosts a website to easily visualize and understand how semantic versions work for real packages: https://semver.npmjs.com[82].

The Risk

With this understanding of semantic versioning, it is clear that the external libraries we use in our project can rapidly change and introduce risks which are both functional issues such as breaking features, or a new bug, as well as new security vulnerabilities.

This is commonly referred to as a **drifting dependencies** problem, and happens quite often.

---

[80] https://docs.npmjs.com/misc/semver
[81] http://semver.org/
[82] https://semver.npmjs.com

The Solution

One simple solution to this problem is to configure npm that upon installing packages it should use a specific range operator that suits your policy, or simply match the exact version that is currently being installed.

This can be achieved from the command-line as well:

```
npm install expressjs --save-exact
```

Another, more standard approach to pinning down package versions is to make use of the shrinkwrap option that npm provides.

To prevent npm from recursively updating nested dependencies, a shrinkwrap creates a map of all installed dependencies, and their dependencies and pins down the exact package versions for the entire dependency tree.

Generating an npm shrinkwrap for a project:

```
npm shrinkwrap
```

The outcome is a JSON file `npm-shrinkwrap.json` which npm will always consult when triggered and follow the package versions for it when installing missing packages. For new packages being installed, it will also update this shrinkwrap file with the exact version to pin it down.

Yarn as npm Package Management

Yarn[83] is a package management client tool for the command line which serves as an alternative to the ubiquitous npm tool.

It's originated from Facebook with the purpose of replacing the npm client tool in order to provide reliable package resolution, and fast installs, as is required with the likes of Facebook's scale.

Characteristics of Yarn

Yarn's advantage can be characterized by the following:

- Reliability and Speed
- Deterministic Package Resolution
- Security

Reliability and Speed

When Yarn downloads packages it always saves them to a local directory so they can be cached locally for offline use. This inherently speeds up the `yarn install` action as there is no bandwidth wasted and one can witness a significantly increased speed when installig modules.

Another optimization step that Yarn is performing is to download packages in parallel rather than serially, one after the other.

 cache for offline
Caching packages means you're easily able to get them when working offline. To find out where exactly Yarn saves them run: `yarn cache dir`

Deterministic Package Resolution

When installing packages using the npm client, it will resolve versions of dependencies in real time. We learned how to handle this problem of drifting dependencies using the npm-shrinkwrap.json methodology. However, the shrinkwrap file has been noted to be problematic in maintaining the dependency graph and reliably resolving pinned version.

---

[83] https://yarnpkg.com

This is where Yarn's method of resolving packages has been improved to become truly deterministic in always resolving to the same version. Yarn generates and maintains it's own yarn.lock file and you aren't expected nor shouldn't be editing it manually. This file is expected to be commited to your code repository so it can be shared with the rest of the team and assure everyone are using the same version of packages across developers, test, and production environments.

Security

Yarn provides security by the means of integrity checking the packages it installs.

When Yarn installs packages it records a SHA1 checksum of the file it downloaded as part of the package information in it's yarn.lock file.

While this is not a means of complete security, it provides safety and validation mechanism where if a man-in-the-middle would be tempering with the packages in transit to send a modified version of the package then Yarn will catch it by noticing the checksum change.

Command Line Usage

It's command line interface is also more restrictive for minimizing human errors. For example, if you were to install the helmet library with npm, it would be possible to easily mistake and install it in the local node_modules/ directory without adding it as a dependency to your project through package.json. Such as:

```
npm install helmet
```

With Yarn, it is impossible to just install a floating module on the project, and the defaults are safe enough to always add your installed module to package.json so you never accidentally push code without the modules it depends on.

Installing Yarn

Yarn can be installed using a variety of options, the easiest of them is using the npm tool itself:

```
npm install -g yarn
```

 Other recommended alternative installation methods include the brew, and curl tools and are documented here: https://yarnpkg.com/en/docs/install

Tracking Dependencies with Yarn

```
yarn outdated
```

Summary

Keeping track of your project's dependency tree is of high importance in order of making sure no vulnerabilities are introduced through 3rd party libraries.

We reviewed a set of tools and techniques to help track them:

- Snyk project is helpful in keeping track of vulnerabilities introduced through your module dependencies, and provides a way to patch your dependencies even if no fix is yet available for them.
- Node Security Platform (nsp) is another useful tool to check for vulnerabilities in 3rd party modules.
- Npm's shrinkwrap method will lock your module dependencies to a specific known version.
- Yarn package manager helps in assuring expected version dependencies

www.ingramcontent.com/pod-product-compliance
Lightning Source LLC
Chambersburg PA
CBHW080933170526
45158CB00008B/2275